FAILURE IS OBSOLETE

Benji Rabhan

FAILURE IS OBSOLETE

The Ultimate Strategy to Create
Recurring Success in Your Business and Your Life

ISBN 978-1-61448-507-0 paperback
ISBN 978-1-61448-508-7 eBook

Blazon Press
an imprint of Morgan James Publishing
The Entrepreneurial Publisher
5 Penn Plaza, 23rd Floor,
New York City, New York 10001
(212) 655-5470 office • (516) 908-4496 fax
www.MorganJamesPublishing.com

Cover design, illustrations, and layout by ClickCore.

My parents, Joe and Bebe Rabhan, for putting up with the frustrating child I know I was and for always loving and supporting me.

My amazingly awesome team at MorrisCore, especially Julie and Pat, for helping me implement more of my ideas, more quickly than I ever could on my own.

Most of all, to my loving wife, Jenna, for continuing to love and support me and for listening to my crazy-sounding theories.

TABLE OF CONTENTS

HOW TO READ THIS BOOK

I have a confession to make. I never really liked reading. To me books take too long to get to the point. They cloud up otherwise great information with too many words. So why would I ever write one?

Great question. The answer is because books are still one of the best ways to get important information into the hands of lots and lots of people for practically nothing, and the information in this book is important. Very important. It could completely change the way you think and make decisions in your business and your everyday life.

For now, I want to do you a favor. I started out by saying I never liked to read. So I want to take the pressure off you. Since this is a book about efficiency and behavior, I've organized it to work for you. No matter what your learning style.

If you love reading books cover to cover — go for it.

If you tend to skip around, reading the stuff that looks interesting — awesome! I like you already.

If you just want to look at the pictures — you'll probably pick up some gems that way too. Or at least I hope you'll be entertained.

How to get the most out of this book:
You should read Chapter One. It lays out the foundation of the Test Before You Test strategy — you'll soon see why I call it the ultimate strategy to create recurring success in your business and your life. Once you understand the

concepts there, you can absorb the rest of the chapters in whatever order you wish. Skip around. Just look at the pictures. Read the first paragraph and the last paragraph. Just read the bolded bits — it's up to you.

I've also included short sidetracks throughout the book. These are resources, sidebars, little things to think about which may or may not have something to do with what's being discussed in the chapter. Feel free to read these as they come along. Or save them all for the end. Or read them all first. Again, it's up to you.

Once you've read chapter one, feel free to explore. However, I do have some recommendations for you:

> If you have a business and want to grow, or if you want to start a business and aren't sure how, check out Section 2: Business

> If you want to learn how to optimize your website for higher conversions, check out Section 3: Your Website.

> If you want to make better and faster decisions in your life and learn how to read other people's behavior, check out Section 4: Life.

Finally, I'll be listing websites, tools, software and other resources throughout. You'll find a handy reference list of all of them on our website. Just visit www.FailureisObsolete.com/reference-list

Okay, enough talk. Let's get going!

So, what's up with the typewriter?

You might have read this book's title and thought, *that's pretty crazy. How can something like failure be obsolete?* I thought the same thing. (That's what made it a good book title.)

The truth is failure isn't completely obsolete. Everyone is going to fail sometimes. I've learned over the years it's important to embrace your failures and learn from them quickly. But, as you'll discover later in this book, I've figured out how to use certain techniques to minimize failure to practically zero. When you can predict a successful outcome to a scenario before it begins, you'll know what to do to eliminate failure. With the way this methodology works, failure really does seem obsolete sometimes.

I've never been a big collector of things. Baseball cards, marbles, stuffed toys — none of the usual childhood things really held my attention. But I do collect typewriters. They have always fascinated me as things of beauty worth preserving. It amazes me to think that typewriters were originally completely mechanical — no electric parts. So much like computers, but without software or code or even a power switch.

When I think of obsolete things, I think of typewriters... so that's what's up with that.

Ready to move forward and learn how to predict success?

I thought so.

1. FAILURE IS WHAT?

What is this all about? Can you really predict success on a reliable basis?

When I was young, everything was an experiment. I was always exploring things; taking them apart; figuring out how they worked - and how they could work for *me*.

> How does the phone work?
> Why does it plug into the wall?
> Where do the wires go?
> How does my voice travel over those wires?
> How can I get a phone in MY room?

These were questions I was asking when I was six. Why did my older sister have a phone in her room when I did not? This was supremely unfair in my six-year-old mind! So, I set out to do something about it — using experimentation. Here's what happened.

It was one of those '90s era phones with a transparent case so you could see all the colored wires and inside workings. She was so proud of it, so naturally I took an interest in it, too. I saw the blue, red, green, and yellow wires and figured out that's what phone wiring was all about.

One day I opened up the phone jack that Lindsey's phone was plugged into. (Yes, I took apart the wall socket.) Inside the jack, I saw the same colored wires, and figured out that was how the phone connected to the outside world. Through these colored wires. Cool! Then I put the wall plate back on and nobody was the wiser.

When I got back to my room, I opened up a flat plate on my wall to see what was inside that one. The same four colored wires all tangled up and shoved back into the wall. Hmm. Interesting.

FIG 1.1: I was always reverse-engineering things to see how they worked. It was my way of experimenting. Using the techniques in this book, you'll be able to reverse-engineer future decisions and events to predict their probability of success or failure.

Through my process of logic and testing, I figured out that I could literally unhook my sister's phone from the wall, rewire the jack, and make it work in my room. And that's what I did. I stole my sister's phone and hooked it up in my room. (Now, the reason I was in that room was because it was little more than a closet. No phone jack, no TV hook-up, nothing. But I was six. My parents figured I didn't need more than that, and they were right. Little did they know, I had other ideas.)

Well, you can imagine what happened that evening. My sister came home and was so angry because I had stolen her phone. My parents were completely confused be-cause they didn't think I had a phone jack in my room.

Where had it come from? They never figured out that I had reached into the wall and rewired my bedroom. And I never told them. Well, not until much later. It's a funny story now, but they wouldn't have been amused when I was six.

The point is I wanted to know everything about everything. So I was always testing things. Experimenting. Reverse-engineering. Testing was my way of exploring the unknown cautiously, a little bit at a time. I could make small leaps of logic, test the effect, and then move forward accordingly.

If I tested connecting the phone wires and they didn't work, then I wouldn't do that again. I'd do something different. Maybe I'd connect them in a different order. Maybe I'd give up on the idea entirely and go take the blender apart.

If I tested my parents' reaction to my "acquiring" my sister's phone and I got away with it, well, what else could I get away with acquiring? The family computer? Maybe.

I had no fear of the consequences because I was making little tests. And, because they were little, I could reverse course quickly before any major damage was done. Also, because they were little, I could make forward progress really fast. Very important in life, as well as in the business world.

This was just how I learned — test, assess, make corrections, test again, correct again. Tiny course corrections meant I ultimately stayed on course to a (usually) successful completion of my goal or task. I didn't want help. I didn't want someone else to tell me his answer. I wanted to figure it out on my own.

I wasn't interested in theories and guesswork and going around an idea the long way. I wanted to know the answer, the *real* answer, as quickly as possible so I could move on to the next cool thing.

That state of mind made school really difficult. It wasn't that I was "lazy" or couldn't focus for long periods of time… wait, no, it was that I couldn't focus for long periods of time. But that wasn't a bad thing. It was just that I saw so many amazing things in the world, and I wanted to experience *all* of them. *Right Now.*

My teachers used to complain that I wasn't "with the class," and they were right. I was far away, in another galaxy — where things moved at my pace.

So what does this have to do with you?
Everything! Because the whole world is becoming completely distractible — like everyone has contracted Attention Deficit Disorder (ADD). It's being forced on us from all sides. Our attention span is about as awesome as a gnat. And it's not our fault.

It's all about speed and volume. It's about how much information you can absorb, and how fast you can absorb it and react to it. Have you watched any TV news channel recently? You're listening to multiple people argue about an issue, while simultaneously watching streaming headlines above and below them. Oh, and we'll throw in a ticking bar with comments on the side. (You know, just in case you get bored.) Oh, and while you're watching, you might also have a laptop or iPad open and a phone to your ear.

Each stream of information ticking by faster than our parents could read. Each stream fighting for our attention. This style of information delivery is all around us. Even when we try to slow down and watch a simple 30-minute sitcom, camera angles change every 5 seconds. And advertising bombards our senses all day, every day, even in our sleep. (Be honest, do you sleep with your cell phone next to your bed?)

—Education is becoming self-guided. (Thank goodness!)
—Technology is developing at mind-bending speed.
—Twitter and texting have reduced our conversations down to 140 abbreviated characters.
—And there's no such thing as a lifetime career anymore. People are expected to switch their line of work an average of seven times.

Whether you like it or not information overload is part of daily life. You can either let it drag you down or you can get excited.

This book is all about my strategy for experimenting. Have you ever heard the saying, "If you must fail, do it quickly and move on"? With this new strategy, you will learn how to experiment and test high-risk ideas in a low-risk environment, practically eliminating the need to fail at all. You will know with almost complete certainty whether an idea will succeed or fail before you invest a lot of time, energy, or money into it.

This strategy is all about getting to the truth of the matter, no matter what the matter is, as quickly as possible. Once you know the truth, you can take the appropriate action to lead you to your goals.

It's also all about risk. Or, more specifically, your risk tolerance. Would you rather bet on a sure thing or go into a risky situation with only a guess as to what's going to happen? The techniques you're going to discover will help you get as close to that sure thing as possible *before* you bet the farm.

People who don't know me very well tend to think I'm a big risk-taker. They see me starting multiple businesses, investing in growth, even skydiving, and they think *he must be some kind of adrenaline junkie.* But really this is just an illusion.

The reality is I hate taking risks. Well, I hate taking risks without a whole lot of confidence that everything is going to turn out in my favor. Even jumping out of a perfectly good airplane didn't seem like a risk to me because I knew the statistics proved that I'd most likely be perfectly fine.

I can trace all this back to two of my childhood mentors, my father, Joe, and my grandfather. They didn't know it at the time, but I watched how they made decisions, what motivated them, and how they invested their time and their money. Their actions shaped how I approached life.

You see, my grandfather was an entrepreneur with a very high risk tolerance. Sometimes things worked out for him, and sometimes they didn't. The high points balanced out the low points for him. I imagine it's the same story for any big risk-taker.

My father, on the other hand, gravitated in the other direction and developed a low risk tolerance. He liked to know the facts, and be sure of how things would turn out.

One of the riskiest financial choices my father ever made was becoming an entrepreneur after a 25-year career in the same large corporation. During those corporate years, he had worked his way up from dishwasher to general manager of a major chain of luxury hotels. Yet he decided to take the leap and opened The Avenue Inn Bed and Breakfast in New Orleans — a gorgeous 1891 Victorian mansion

FIG 1.2: Proprietors Joe and Bebe Rabhan welcome guests to The Avenue Inn Bed & Breakfast in New Orleans, LA. (http://www.avenueinnbb.com/)

with 17 bedrooms, right on the streetcar line.

Starting your own business is a major investment of time, energy, and money, especially in the hotel space. It was extremely risky to do what he did. And, until recently, I thought it was very out of character for him. It kind of baffled me how he managed to take such a big step when he normally preferred safer waters.

Now that I look back at those days through the filter of my own choices, I can see that he was able to do it because he had confidence in his experience and his knowledge of the industry. And he had every right to be confident. He knew he would succeed, so it didn't seem so risky. Knowing that now, I probably would have made the same choice if I had been in his position.

That decision paid off for our family. The Avenue Inn Bed and Breakfast survived the tourism crash after 9/11, Hurricane Katrina, and the terrible economic climate of the past several years for two simple reasons, my father's creativity and his expertise in the industry. Because of this, my father and mother still welcome guests today. In fact, the business is doing better than ever. It turned out to be a great move for our family. It was a risk, but a calculated one.

Both these men had great influence on my life, though they probably didn't know it (until they read this book). I saw the positive and the negative sides of both the high-risk and low-risk lifestyles. I didn't want to be exactly like either of them; I wanted the best of both worlds. I wanted to have the excitement and reward of risk, but only if I knew it was a sure thing. That sounds like an impossible task, doesn't it? Well, it doesn't have to be!

Isn't that what we all want, at least some of the time? To be fairly sure our ventures and ideas are going to turn out in our favor?

Combining my father and grandfather's influence with my natural inclination to experiment and reverse-engineer things helped me come up with the strategies I use every day. You're going to learn to use some of those strategies.

As a child, I was envious of my grandfather's entrepreneurial spirit. But I grew up mostly like my dad. I choose to make my decisions and take risks based on facts, not wild guesses, unknowns, or promises.

Why should you care about this stuff?
The point is people aren't waiting around until half their lives have gone by to figure out how to succeed. We're taught to start setting goals and dreams for ourselves in kindergarten, but we aren't really taught how to make those goals and dreams happen quickly. We're told to "work hard" and "keep at it" and eventually we'll get what we want. Maybe.

Yeah. I'm not very good at waiting. If it's not going to happen, I'd rather move on.

So I consciously decided to get a lifetime of experience in as little time as possible. Fast. Like life. So I could put more life into my years and really LIVE. And if you're reading this book, I think you've probably made a similar choice; or at least you dream about it.

Did you know more and more teenagers are becoming millionaires these days? They don't want to wait until they "grow up" and "climb the corporate ladder" to be successful. And they don't have to. Thanks to the speed of technology and freedom of information, they can do what they want, when they want to, where they want to —and be more successful than their parents or grandparents ever dreamed possible.

Kids are being handed iPads before they can even form sentences. The whole world is at their fingertips before they reach preschool. Facts, figures, and formulas are available to them anytime. Slowly, but surely, education is shifting. In the next 15 years, it will be a very different experience than what any of us had before technology was so common in life and schools.

The world is changing! You can get ahead or get left behind. Don't want to wind up working for your grandchildren? Then learn this stuff now. Because those tots are not going to wait until they graduate college before they change the world. They're going to do it much sooner. And

FIG 1.3: The future will move at the speed of thought. There's no time to wait around hoping for the best when you can predict successful outcomes before you start. It doesn't matter what decision you need to make, this strategy will help you make it quickly and with confidence.

you can label them ADHD, you can feed them drugs to slow them down, but in the end, they are the future. And the future will move at the speed of thought.

I think the older you are the harder it is to believe that a 12-year-old can start up a new business and leave you in the dust. But it's true. It happens everyday.

The good news is you can do it, too, with the right frame of mind and some good strategy behind you.

Want proof? I can give you many examples. I'm actually one of them. At age 11, I was already dreaming of my first company, and even built a website for it. It was called Silver Wizard, Inc. Even though the company was imaginary, we had a real website.

I built my first ecommerce website for a client at the age of 13. I've started or partnered in dozens of businesses — some were successful, some weren't. But I consciously cataloged the lessons learned from each one, and used those lessons to make the next one better. I've had tons of experiences crammed into a short span of time, leaving (hopefully) many productive years ahead to build more and more successes. I've got friends younger than me making millions of dollars with their ideas...and they're only getting started.

Take my friend, Emerson Spartz, for example. He built a small Harry Potter fan website when he was 12 years old. Today MuggleNet is the most successful Harry Potter site on the web. Even with the final books and movies long since past, the site continues as a thriving community of fans. They publish comprehensive reference books, post stories and artwork; and J.K. Rowling herself has been known to pop in now and then (though she never announces herself.) Spartz Media is now one of the fastest growing digital media publishers worth millions of dollars.

More and more young people are starting businesses and getting those first awkward mistakes out of the way very early in life. Which means by the time they reach 19 or 20, they are serious competition for anyone else in their industry.

An eight-year-old can build a website that makes money. That's the easy part. The hard part is making sound decisions with clarity and speed. It's that clarity and speed that separates successful businesses (and successful lives) from the less successful ones.

FIG 1.4: Today's kids aren't afraid to experiment with business ideas, and some of them are succeeding big-time.

The old way of thinking was that it takes years or even decades of experience before you know enough to make good decisions and be successful. It was called "paying your dues."

With modern technology and the techniques I'm going to explain, you can make the right decision in as little as a few minutes.

People today are so bombarded with information that they get paralyzed. They live in fear of making the wrong decision, so instead they make NO decision. You're going to have a methodical way to figure out the best option as quickly as you can, especially when you're faced with an eternity of options.

I want to give you a glimpse into the future and help you succeed there. This is how you can make decisions faster, based on reality, instead of guesswork or biased interpretation.

How this methodology got started
When I was a kid, they tested my learning style, and I scored evenly across audio, visual, and kinesthetic learning. I was different, and that was good (at least to me). This meant I was free to develop my own learning style. I didn't think much of it while growing up, but now I realize I wound up developing the strategies you're about to discover.

This learning style was just how I lived my life. I didn't think it was anything special until I started paying attention to other people. This was NOT how they lived their lives, and they experienced needless wasted time and effort taking the slow way around things. When friends asked me for advice, I could almost always come up with a way to circumvent the problem and wind up with a successful outcome in half the time.

It doesn't matter what your goals are - a successful business, a blissful marriage, a great relationship with your kids — the ultimate goal is happiness, right? In the end, we all just want to be happy. So why do we make it so difficult? (I don't know. That's the subject of another book.)

👍 GOOD TO KNOW

The Trend Toward Teen Entrepreneurs

When 13-year-old Hart Main saw his sister selling scented candles as a fundraiser, he thought, *why aren't there any manly-scented candles* (think fresh-cut grass, leather, bacon, and grandpa's pipe). So, he started up his own company called ManCan. The candles are made inside recycled soup cans. With thousands of candles sold in over 60 shops nationwide, the little company that started as a joke is growing by leaps and bounds. www.man-cans.com

Kids aren't waiting to grow up before doing cool things with their lives. Thanks to the speed of developing technology and the amazing amounts of free information available on the Internet, they don't have to.

If you're old enough to read, and curious enough to try things without fear of making mistakes — you can start a business. Whether you succeed or fail at those early efforts doesn't matter, because the sooner you start making mistakes and learning from them, the sooner you succeed.

The thing about kids is they aren't afraid to try things. There's little perceived risk on their part. If they try programming their own video game and it doesn't work — so what?

They can try it again, or try something else. The fun, creativity, and learning come first. The business comes second.

What does this mean for older generations? It means we have to think and move faster!

Young start-ups can compete with and overtake long-established businesses simply by being nimble, quick to implement, and quick to react to constant change.

 For more information, check out
<u>www.FailureisObsolete.com/teen-entrepreneurs</u>

THINGS TO REMEMBER

_____
_____
_____
_____
_____
_____
_____
_____
_____
_____
_____
_____
_____
_____
_____
_____
_____

2. WHAT IS TEST BEFORE YOU TEST?

How to use this strategy to be more successful, more often.

The strategy you're about to learn is what I call Test *Before* You Test. Testing theories and experimenting are important activities because they give us clues toward making successful decisions.

We all want to succeed. Whether it's succeeding on an exam in school, succeeding in the business world, on the soccer field, or in the dating arena, success makes us feel good and moves us forward on our journey.

Success depends on us making good decisions. Over and over again. When we inevitably make a bad decision, our future success depends on us recovering quickly and changing course before we get bogged down in the consequences of the bad decision. Or worse, we get so discouraged that we simply don't make any more decisions at all.

So how do we know which decisions are good ones and which aren't? How do we know a good idea from a bad one?

We base all our decisions on data.
That could be data we've collected ourselves through experience; data others have collected and recorded; and data

we collect in the moment as the decision is playing out.

Many of us also base our decisions on our desires or by guessing.
Our imaginations are powerful. If we are presented with two options, our imaginations can run dozens of scenarios for how these options will play out in reality. The rational mind then chooses the most likely outcomes based on prior experience, and we take our best guess as to which option to choose.

In reality, all our decisions are based on using our best guess.
Unless you're a time traveler, you can't truly know what the outcome of a decision will be unless you have test data to back you up. The more data we have *before* we make a decision, the more likely we'll make the correct choice. And the more successful we'll be.

How do we gather that data? We gather it through testing and real world experience (ours or someone else's).

We test all the time, whether we know it or not.
Testing is how we make decisions about everything.

> Do you turn left or turn right?
> Do you stop or go?
> Do I finish writing this chapter or break for an early lunch and return to it this afternoon?

Unconsciously, we run little test scenarios in our heads based on data we've already collected through prior experience.

Do you turn left or right? Well, the data we already have tells us if we go left, we'll get closer to our final destination, home. And if we go right, we'll be farther away. So, we naturally go left.

But what if we don't have that data? What if we're lost? We have to collect more data to help us make the decision. We look at a map or turn on the GPS. Before satellite technology, maps were made by people and were based on recorded experiences. They have been proven reliable in the past, so we feel confident using them in this situation.

Do you stop or go? Well, the previous data collected through decades of experience says if the light is red and we go, it's very possible we'll have an accident. Better stop until the light turns green.

The data also says it's too early for lunch, and I'm on a roll writing this. So, I'm better off continuing while I have the thoughts in my head. Once I'm finished, I can treat myself to a leisurely meal on the deck.

FIG 2.1: Prior experience tells me I should finish working on this chapter and then enjoy a nice lunch on the deck. Decisions don't have to be based on guessing. They can be based on prior experience or new data.

This is obvious. Our brains do it without thinking most of the time whenever we're presented with a decision to make. Our brains are testing machines. Once we've gathered enough data from enough similar tests to predict a successful outcome every time, that behavior becomes a habit.

I've found there are three types of traditional testing:

1. Trial and Error — This is also called the "spaghetti method." You just throw stuff at the wall and see what sticks. You have an idea, and you try it. Either you succeed or you don't. When you record the results or add it to your mental database of experience, you can use trial and error as data gathering for future ideas. Trial and error can work, but it's slow, unpredictable, and terribly inefficient.

2. Scientific Method — This a lot like trial and error, just more evolved. You define a hypothesis (make a guess), run an experiment, and see if you were right. Usually, whether the test works or doesn't is irrelevant. Either way, you are gathering data. Unfortunately, the data gathering can go on indefinitely. Most of the time, you'll need to run many more tests to rule out other possibilities.

This is smarter than straight trial and error but complicated and risky, and it's still a guessing game. Experimenting is very important and everyone should be doing it, especially in business. But it's still based on guessing, then experimenting to see if your guess was right or wrong. And your results are based on how well you defined the problem to begin with. There's got to be a faster, more reliable way to get at the right answer.

3. Surveys — These are great for collecting lots of data, and there are innovative ways to use surveys. For a long time, surveys have been considered one of the best ways for businesses to get the data they need to make smarter decisions about consumers, predicting behavior, or how to invest money. Unfortunately, surveys are error prone and can be very expensive. The more there is at stake, the more expensive the survey will be. (Fortune 500 companies pay hundreds of thousands of dollars to run focus groups and acquire survey data for fairly simple questions.)

The main problem with surveys and focus groups is they are not reliable. People will say one thing and do another — not because they are trying to be misleading (usually), but because they truly believe what they're saying. They don't even realize that the choices they think they make are not always accurate.

👍 GOOD TO KNOW

We Aren't Good Judges of Our Own Behavior.

According to the psychological theory of self-perception, we are terrible at judging our "true selves". The way we think we look is rarely the truth. The way we believe we act is often not reality.

We all believe we behave a certain way in public and have consistent, predictable buying behaviors. But objective observation with video cameras, and consumer tracking through things like grocery store membership cards, prove that we often act completely different than we think we do. In other words, we can't always count on the way we "think" we are. Objective testing is a better way to get reliable data you can count on.

It's not a bad thing; it's just human behavior. We deceive ourselves all the time, creating imagined self-images and behaviors based on our own sets of rules and morals.

An extreme example of this would be someone

with an eating disorder. No matter how thin the cameras, the scales, and the doctors say they are, the individual truly believes they are fat. They can see it in the mirror, even though everyone else sees something completely different.

For more information, check out
www.FailureisObsolete.com/self-perception

Flip through any issue of *Journal of Marketing Research* or *Journal of the American Statistical Association* (or really any serious marketing journal) and you'll see that researchers are continually seeking better ways to measure consumer behavior. Why? Because surveys are inherently flawed. The data doesn't always tell the truth, and even when it does, the truth can change from day to day.

Recent technology breakthroughs allow marketers to track purchasing behavior on a granular level. They know everything you bought at the grocery store last week, how often you buy gasoline (and what brand). They even know when big life events are happening like weddings, your first child, and milestone birthdays. While all this technology is great, it's often out of reach for most businesses. They are still forced to rely on flawed surveys or just plain guessing to figure out what their customers really want.

Are surveys worthwhile? Sometimes. Surveys can point you in the right direction, but they may not be conclusive and may even be misleading. The most common problem I've found with business surveys is they are surveying their customers instead of prospects. This skews the data in the wrong direction.

Is a survey worth hundreds of thousands of dollars? Maybe. Is there a better and cheaper way to get more conclusive data? Often, the answer is yes.

In my life, there's a #4 — Test Before You Test

TBYT adds a new dimension to these testing methods so you know certain data ahead of time. This way, when you go through the real test of an idea, you're not guessing at the outcome — you're simply confirming it. The rate of successful outcomes for testing before you test is far better than testing by trial and error, or basing decisions on research methods like surveys.

Certain industries use this idea all the time. For example, car manufacturers use computer simulators to test out risky new ideas in a low-risk environment. They can test out wind resistance, speed tolerance, safety features, and other ideas, which lead to innovations and better vehicles. And they can test it all out before they ever build the first prototype.

So how does TBYT work anyway?
Let's say you had an idea for a new product — let's say it's a new kind of plant food. It's guaranteed to grow big, beautiful tomatoes with no toxic residue that could endanger people or pets. Sounds like a great business idea, right?

FIG 2.2: Test your business idea before you sink a lot of time and money into it. Are the customers really there? Or are you just hoping they'll be there?

The trial and error methodology would tell you to create the product — including all the manufacturing, storage, shipping, branding, labeling, advertising and everything else that goes along with creating a product. Then try to sell it. If you make a lot of money — woohoo! You're a success. If you go bankrupt — bummer. That's not a very smart way to run a business, yet people do it all the time.

Now, if you were a large corporation with lots of money to put into research and development, market research, and advertising, you could probably handle the risk associated with trial and error. If you lose a bundle, it's just the cost of doing business. Or maybe it's worth a million dollars of surveys and market research to simply get better data.

But what if you're an entrepreneur who just stumbled across this magic concoction that grows huge tomato plants. You think it could be an amazingly successful plant food, but you don't have a lot of money to invest in developing it. Plus, you work full time, and this is just a little hobby project. If you knew it was likely to succeed, you'd pour your heart and soul into it. But you're just not sure.

If you're in that situation, you definitely want to test before you test! Using TBYT allows you to determine the likelihood of success for your new plant food before you spend all the time and money involved in making and marketing the product.

It lets you pick the winners — almost every time.

So how would you go about using the TBYT method to decide if you should move forward with this idea? Well, let's say you're a member of a large regional garden club, and they have an email newsletter that goes out to hundreds of gardeners each week. Every issue has one or two cool new product reviews for items people can purchase online.

You *could* make up some of your magic plant food and try to sell it to the subscribers. That would be testing using trial and error.

You could make up a survey and ask people whether they would be interested in buying a product like yours. But we already know people rarely act the way they say they will.

So, instead, you create a quick web page advertising the product (with lots of pictures of you and your gorgeous tomatoes) and include a button that says "Order Now." Then you get permission from the editor to run an article about how you discovered this cool new formula and how awesome your tomatoes were last year. Then you add in a link that takes them to the web page advertising your product. Finally, you just count the number of people who click the "Order Now" button. You don't even need to build the order system or shopping cart yet because that's not necessary to get the answer you want. All you're doing is counting how many people click "Order Now."

That's testing *before* you test. You didn't have to create any product. All you did was spend a few hours building a web page and writing an article. You collected a high-level of reliable data (people who would actually buy your product) for very low risk (no money, and just a little time.)

Now, you might be thinking, "what about the people who clicked the order button?" Won't they be angry that there was no product to buy? No. Because you were smart and created another page that read "This product is coming soon. Sign up here with your name and email to be notified when it's ready." This way you collected your data and a list of potential customers you can sell to when you're ready.

TBYT is all about gathering data involving actual behavior in the most low-risk, low-cost way possible. So you can pre-prove that your idea has legs without going through the time and expense of carrying out the entire idea to see if it's successful.

Proving real behavior — not filtered behavior.
Hopefully, I've made this clear by now... **People rarely act in reality the way they say they would on a survey or in a focus group.**

Testing before you test means you are testing to determine real behavior, not filtered or perceived behavior, or imagined scenarios.
You're not "asking" consumers which toothpaste they prefer. You're following them down the toothpaste aisle and seeing which one they actually buy.

FIG 2.3: Test Before You Test is the next best thing to having your own personal marketing ninjas follow customers around to see what brands they *actually* consider and buy.

You're not asking whether your friends "think" your business idea is a good one. You're setting up a web page and seeing if anyone is actually willing to buy your amazing new plant food.

Behavioral context is the key to setting up a good Test Before You Test.

Before we delve into all the ways you can use TBYT to speed up your success in life and business, you need to understand one important concept — what I call *behavioral context*. Here's a simple formula to remember.

Same Audience + Same Action =
Same Behavioral Context

Anytime you're designing a TBYT scenario, you're looking for similar behavioral context in the scenarios. You want to discover how a certain audience will act in one high-risk situation by testing the same audience in a lower-risk situation where the desired action is the same, or as close as possible.

How can a dentist use TBYT?

Let's look at an example. Let's say you're a dentist thinking about whether you want to begin offering a new teeth whitening service to your patients. (I don't know anything about being a dentist — this is all hypothetical!)

Let's say it's expensive (high-risk) to get all the equipment, supplies, and training you need to get started, and you're just not sure if your patients will buy the service from you.

After all, they can just go to the grocery store and buy a cheap whitening kit to use at home.

To design a TBYT for this situation, you need to figure out the behavioral context. Here's how you do it:

Step 1: What's the audience?
Your existing patients

Step 2: What's the behavior you want to test?
Purchasing a teeth whitening package in the office

Trial and Error Method: Most dentists would feel they need to get all the training, equipment, and supplies before advertising the service. They would prepare the service, and then hope for the best.

TBYT scenario: Advertise the service and see if anyone requests an appointment. If they do, keep a list and tell them they will be the first to get scheduled when you're ready to accept appointments.

It's important in this case that you keep the variables in the TBYT as close as possible to the real situation. If you would normally advertise with flyers in your waiting room and a special notice on the home page of your website, then use those methods for the TBYT.

If you would normally advertise with a poster in your waiting room, but you don't use that method for the TBYT, your results will be skewed. You may still get enough signups to move forward with the expense of the training and equipment, but the poster may give you better data because it's your normal means of communication.

FIG 2.4: If you would normally advertise a new service with a poster in your waiting room, do the same for your TBYT scenario to keep the audience consistent.

Remember, keep your behavioral context as close as possible for both the TBYT and the real situation. The outside details, like what actual tooth whitening technique you're going to offer, don't really matter if you weren't going to use it in your advertising anyway.

Here's a slightly different example.

How can an eCommerce site use TBYT?

Let's say you sell outdoor gear and camping supplies online. You're thinking about building an extensive new website just for fishing fanatics. You love the look of your competitor's website — it's primarily green and does a lot of business. Your designer thinks a yellow site would work better for your audience. Do you go with green or yellow?

FIG 2.5: This is a screenshot from a business similar to the example. Would it sell better in green or yellow? TBYT gives you the answer before you spend the time and money for a new site. (SierraTradingPost.com)

When it comes to websites, most business owners go with what they think is "pretty." But which color scheme will actually convert more visitors into paying customers? Which one will have the best conversion rate? (A conversion rate is the percentage of visitors to your website that take a certain action. In this case, the action is making a purchase. We'll get into this concept in greater detail later.)

Most people would simply build and launch that pretty new site and hope for the best. Conversion experts would launch the new site as a test, split the traffic between the new and old sites, and compare the results. After all, conversion rates are the bottom line here. But you're still running a high-stakes, expensive test. What if the new site fails to outperform the old site? You've spent a lot of time and money.

Let's run a TBYT scenario *before* you spend a lot of time and money building a site that doesn't have the best conversion rate.

Step 1: What's the audience?
Fishing fanatics on your mailing list.

Step 2: What's the behavior you want to test?
Buying fishing supplies on a website. Which converts better - green or yellow?

TBYT scenario: Assuming you have a decent sized email list, split your list in half. Send one half a green version of a newsletter and the other half a yellow version. Include prominent links to fishing gear on your current website. Determine if the number of clicks is greater on the green or the yellow newsletter.

You already have a list of camping fans, some of them buy fishing supplies from you. So by sending a green email newsletter to half your list and a yellow one to the other half, you can determine which color attracts the most clicks on fishing gear advertisements.

The fact that your website is the same old one doesn't matter. You're testing the audience (your list) and the behavior (clicking on green or yellow).

This is an example of classic A/B split-testing that we do for online businesses all the time. Conversion rate optimization is the practice of continually improving and testing a new version of something against an old version. The goal is to find improvements that boost the conversion rate. We are never done testing. There are always improvements we can make.

Sometimes the results of split testing are dramatic, with a clear winner and a clear loser. Sometimes there is no clear winner, and you are left with more questions than answers. In the case of the fishing gear, it's possible the yellow version could outperform the green by 10 to 1. Or it's also possible they produce the exact same results. In which case, you either perform a slightly different test, or you determine that the color really doesn't matter and go with what looks best to your eye. Either way, you haven't blown $5,000 on a new website that's the wrong color. And, you didn't make a guess, you tested.

IMPORTANT: *Split testing is different than Test Before You Test. If it's confusing, we'll go over the difference in more detail later on.*

Let's use the above example of the website for a moment.

Technically, we are split testing the email list. We split the audience in half and test how they behave.

However, most people would use the trial and error method of building the new website first and then split testing it. This is high risk. There's a lot of money and time at stake. By running a Test Before You Test scenario in which you split test an *already existing* newsletter, you are lowering the risk to almost nothing and gathering valuable data about your audience's behavior.

I call it Test *Before* You Test because the "real" test will come later — if and when you build the new website. The TBYT is giving you assurances that you are doing the right thing. It's helping you predict success or failure before you spend a lot of time and money.

In both the dentist and the fishing examples, you were looking for the likely behavioral outcome. The audience needs to be the same, and the action or behavior needs to be the same. In this case, the details (a website or a newsletter) don't matter because...

> Same Audience + Same Action =
> ## Same Behavioral Context

Minimize Risk - Maximize Positive Results.
Testing before you test means you're lowering your risk of spending lots of time, energy, and money only to have the idea fail. It lets you know which option to choose, what changes to make, or whether it's even worth making a change in the first place. It lets you predict the outcome of almost any situation *before* you're in the actual situation.

What you're going to learn in the rest of this book is how to structure TBYT scenarios to answer more complicated problems and move you closer to your goals as fast as possible. You're also going to discover how even failed tests give you valuable data you can use to make your next decision more successful.

Living your life from the TBYT perspective means you test everything on purpose. Another way to think about it is to consciously test to determine the correct path, before you start on the journey.

It may seem that setting up tests to predetermine outcomes is taking the long way around the problem. Why not just give it your best guess and then wait to find out whether you succeed or fail?

Because of the wait time.

How many failures do you have to wait through before you get a success? And how long do your ideas take to come to fruition? And how much time, energy, and money will you be wasting in all this time when you could have just reverse-engineered the desired result, set up a data gathering test, and made the correct decision the first time?

By testing your way to success, you get where you want to go much faster and with much lower risk. And if you're racing against time, the economy, or a competitor, that's a huge advantage.

This is one of the reasons most business start-ups fail so miserably. They spend enormous amounts of time and money on a hunch or an idea. Then wait for it to play out to see if it was a success. In today's world where life moves at the speed of thought, that's just too slow.

Why Lincoln Was Wrong

Abraham Lincoln was a great president and obviously an intelligent person. But I remember a quote attributed to him that said something like, "If I've got one hour to chop down a tree, I'm going to spend the first 45 minutes sharpening the axe."

Here's what I would do instead:

FIG 2.6: Lincoln said it's all about preparation. If you have one hour to chop down a tree, spend 45 minutes sharpening the axe. I say it's all about certainty of success and optimizing my time.

That's smart, right? It is, but I see that as an older way of thinking and too risky. When I heard this quote from him, it just didn't sit right with me for some reason. I just didn't agree with his strategy.

If I had to chop down a tree and the tree was important, I'd sharpen the axe for 10 minutes and try it on a smaller tree to see how much sharper I needed it. Then I would sharpen until I was positive it could knock down the big tree in as few swipes as possible.

I may even finish before the hour is up and can go grab a beer. With Lincoln's strategy, what if 15 minutes isn't enough time no matter how sharp the axe is? Now you're out of time.

It's a different way of approaching the issue, but the guy who sharpened for 45 minutes may have wasted a lot of time and energy — and there's still no guarantee he will be able to cut the tree down in that last 15 minutes.

That's the advantage of Test Before You Test. It's a shortcut to certain success.

Of course, this is all hypothetical. These days what I'd *really* do is find a lumberjack online and hire him to do the work with a chainsaw while I go enjoy my beer!

THINGS TO REMEMBER

GOALS & ACTIONABLES

TBYT PRACTICE SHEET

Audience:

_____

_____

_____

_____

Action:

_____

_____

_____

_____

Test:

_____

_____

_____

_____

_____

_____

_____

_____

3. BUSINESS

How to use the Test Before You Test strategy to make better, more profitable decisions in your business — whether you're just starting out, or have a multimillion-dollar company.

Creative ideas for new businesses seem to be everywhere.

You get a great idea for a new transportation system driving to work. You figure out the key to your new product delivery system over lunch with a co-worker. Your evening workout brings a flood of great new services you can offer without raising overhead.

For certain people, the entrepreneurial spirit and innovative ideas are almost an addiction. They are always on the lookout for the next big idea. It's exciting to turn one little spark of imagination into a huge success.

FIG 3.1: It's easy to get carried away with your great ideas. Don't throw away good money on high-risk scenarios! Use low-risk testing first to practically guarantee success.

Yet a fairly high percentage of small businesses ulti-mately fail. Why? Because they're doing something wrong. Something wasn't thought out all the way. Or there was a blind spot in the plan, a major flaw they didn't see.

But how do you know what that flaw is? If you're having awesome ideas all the time, how can you pick the winners from the losers?

You could just move ahead with the idea you think has the most merit and hope for the best. Or you can prove or dis-prove the business concept first with a fast, low-risk, data-gathering Test Before You Test (TBYT) scenario focusing on the correct behavioral context. If that idea doesn't pan out, then you can quickly modify it or move to the next idea. You haven't spent months or years laboring away on a dream that's not going to work in the long run.

Starting a business means taking risks; but you can lower your risk significantly using the TBYT strategy. I'm not a high-risk personality. Gambling with an un-known outcome is just too much for me. But I do love tak-ing big, calculated risks. When I get a business idea, I want to be as sure as I can of a success before I'll invest a lot of time and money. In other words, I use the Test Before You Test methodology to get the highest proof of concept before going full speed ahead on a particular venture.

It wasn't always that way, though. I learned this lesson the hard way, by taking lots of unnecessary risks and using the trial and error method of business. Fortunately, most of my risks were relatively small. So my failures may have stung a little, but they weren't crippling.

Once, I made a huge bet on a business idea without testing

it first. Even though it was profitable, I consider it a failure overall. Here's what happened:

Many years ago, I was brought this amazing idea for running a mobile car detailing service. I called it Wash Me Mobile. I thought I had all the angles worked out. Almost every other mobile detailing company in the nation was limited because they had just one truck with a huge water tank on the back. Carrying water around was expensive, and you needed special equipment. Their model wasn't scalable; it was usually just one guy and his truck. We thought we could do better.

We contracted with a company in Australia that sold waterless car washing products so we didn't need to haul a water tank all over town. In fact, we got it down to where our employees could carry everything they needed for the job in the back of their own car.

We built the whole model around scalability because we could hire almost anyone to do the job. And the best part was we would automate almost the whole administrative process by using online ordering and a custom-built order management system.

The idea was that people would come to our website and schedule one-time or recurring detailing sessions online. They could order special services, make comments, and manage everything right from their computer. Then our system would automatically assign our employees their jobs for the day. They could just print out their work orders and head out to handle the jobs. Our system would tell us when we needed to hire more people, order more products, everything was automated!

It was such a slick system. We spent four or five months and thousands of dollars developing the fancy coding needed to run a complex website like this. We had everything on a high-margin model, and we really thought we had a winner. We had a completely automated customer management (CRM) system in the back end, clients could see before and after pictures of their cars — it really was an awesome piece of work.

We were profitable, and from the outside, it looked great. But we closed after about six months of starting the business. Why? There were a couple of reasons. The first reason being that any time you are bootstrapping a business, you have to be willing to do all the jobs yourself. Once summer hit in Florida, nobody wanted to be out in the hot sun scrubbing cars. I wound up having to do the work myself, and quickly got tired of it.

But that's not the real reason it ended. It's just what forced me to make a decision and reflect upon what got me there. The real inherent flaw in the business was that we spent so much money and time building the website (which is the part I loved the most) without testing the online ordering concept. The fact was that, at the time, no one in our market even thought about ordering car detailing online. So we didn't have enough web traffic to make the concept work. (Today it would work like a dream in some cities, but I've moved on.)

The same thing happened in the pizza industry. When they started online ordering, it was very rare for anyone to order something like that online. Pizza companies spent a lot of money and time on the same idea we had. Even though people could order online, they still just picked up the phone and called in their order.

We could have done a survey about online ordering and asked people if they would use a website to schedule an appointment, and it's likely the pizza companies did just that. It's also likely that people said, "Sure, we'd use that!" But as we know, people don't behave the way they say they will. The ironic part about the pizza example is people would go to the website to look up the phone number — and *still* call in the order!

So what can we learn from the car wash example? What's the big lesson? We should have run a TBYT to test the online ordering idea before we spent all that time and money.

FIG 3.2: Lesson learned — when you're bootstrapping, always be willing to do the lowliest job in the company yourself.

We could have set up a very simple one-page website with an online order button right next to the phone number. Then we would have counted how many people clicked the order online button. (If anyone did click to order online, we would have a simple message that read, "Coming soon — please call".)

Instead of spending thousands and thousands of dollars developing a system no one really used, we would have changed the model or moved on to something more promising.

Remember:

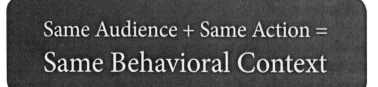

Same Audience + Same Action =
Same Behavioral Context

So by using flyers around town and in prominent office complexes (audience) and asking them to go to a website and click a button (action), we would have gathered significant data about their behavior.

That data would have shown us that the business could be a great success if we used old-fashioned flyers, a dedicated phone line, and offline media instead of building that huge website. But because we didn't take that data-gathering step, we didn't figure out the correct marketing scheme until we were already burned out and deep in debt.

As I was sitting there in the 110-degree heat scrubbing cars, I was thinking, what could I have done differently? How can I apply that so I never make this mistake again? I was determined to learn the lesson I needed to learn. Learn it ONCE and get on with my next business.

That lesson was test. Test often. Test everything. Make sure you're going to be successful before you invest the time and money. This is when the Test Before You Test strategy really solidified in my mind as a concept.

What does this mean for you? Use TBYT scenarios to prove or disprove your concept before you start a business or run with an idea.

Let's look at Facebook for a moment.
Mark Zuckerberg had an idea, and he ran with it. And it was a huge, if accidental, success. But let's imagine for a moment he did a survey first.

"Hello ma'am, could you tell me if you would ever share intimate details about your life, like your birthdate and location at any given moment, on a website? Would you also include pictures and videos of your friends and family on that website? And would you share those things knowing that anyone in the entire world could view them — including government agencies, your boss, future employers, and the police? Oh, and would you mind if we tracked all the things you like and don't like and use the data for marketing purposes so we can sell you stuff?"

FIG 3.3: Who in his right mind would have told a surveyor , *"Sure, I'd love to share all my most intimate moments, embarrassing pictures, and personal information like my birthday with the whole world. Sign me up"?* But when Facebook came around, nearly a billion of us did sign up. Didn't you?

Almost no one in his right mind would have said, "Yes, sure, go ahead. That sounds great!" to questions like that. And yet people are doing these things every second of every day right now on Facebook and other social media sites. Surveys don't provide reliable information about our behavior.

Yet Zuckerberg did run a kind of test. He built a similar version of the basic Facebook concept on a much simpler website to see if college students would post their information.

(I remember it because I was in college at the time, and we were members of the same fraternity organization. I remember thinking it wouldn't last because I couldn't understand why anyone would want to do this. But I was wrong — always gather the data.)

This just goes to prove that often really successful people *accidentally* use the Test Before You Test strategy. They aren't doing it *on purpose*; it's just what happens in the evolution of an idea. Facebook was tested small and then evolved into this crazy-huge thing that's changing the way we live our lives.

You can do this, too, but on purpose!
If you have a big business idea, you don't need to go out and get huge investors, build the whole thing, and hope for the best. Build a test version with similar behavioral context to test the idea in a low-risk setting. You have the advantage over Facebook because you can use the Test Before You Test strategy *on purpose*.

HOW TO USE TEST BEFORE YOU TEST TO DEVELOP A PRODUCT OR SERVICE

Similar to testing a business idea or concept, you can use a data-gathering TBYT to prove or disprove a concept for a new product or service you may be thinking of offering in your current business.

Conventional wisdom would say, "build it and they will come." But we know that's not always the case. Very oten businesses will offer the wrong products to the wrong customers. Or, maybe it's the right product, but it's not as good as it could be. Maybe it's missing a major feature, or has too many bells and whistles. Too much can be as bad as too little.

Product development is one area where surveys are used a lot. You put an idea forward to your market, ask them if they would buy it, what features they would like added, etc. Then tally up the results and build the product accordingly. But that's almost as dangerous as just building it blindly. Why? Because surveys don't always depict accurate behavior.

By using Test Before You Test to determine actual behavior, you will have a much better picture of what your product should look like or whether you should build it at all.

The idea here is to build the offer as a concept to see if people are interested enough to order it. If so, then you move ahead. If you don't get enough interest, you modify the offer, or scrap it altogether (and smile either way).

Do some of the marketing first. Gather pre-orders or levels of interest. Then build the product.

One way to do this is to use a landing page on the Internet. (A landing page in this case is a single page that lays out the whole offer or product and includes an order button.)

Remember the formula:

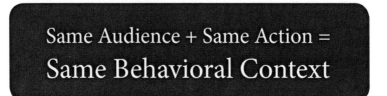

Same Audience + Same Action =
Same Behavioral Context

So you would need the audience for your TBYT scenario to be the same as the audience you would expect to buy the real thing. (Another word for online audience is "traffic".) What traffic streams will you be using for the real offer? Pay-per-click ads? Social media? Flyers? Newspaper ads? Keep your traffic as cheap as possible to minimize risk, but try to make it as close to the real thing as you can.

The action for the TBYT needs to match the real thing, too. So, if you plan to sell this product online, using an "order now" button on a landing page is fine. But if your customers will have to call you to place the order, your test should have a phone number, even if it just tracks the calls and goes directly to a "coming soon" voicemail.

Make sure you don't anger your customers by not delivering something they think they ordered. Always add a "coming soon" notice after they click or call. And let them know you appreciate their interest, and they will be the first to know when it's available. This way, you're building up excitement and a pre-qualified list of potential customers.

Information marketers do this kind of testing all the time. But some abuse it, and care more about selling the product than making something people can really use and benefit from. They focus on the selling first and then build useless products after the fact just because they have cash in hand. It's dishonest, and I strongly disagree with abusing the concept this way.

If you're like me, you're going to want to focus on building a really excellent product or service, and your testing will always be done with integrity. People will appreciate that you're taking the time to find out what they really want before you try to sell them another "widget."

Remember the dentist from the earlier example? He was wondering if he should start offering a teeth whitening service. After all, they may not want to pay for professional whitening. His patients could just use an in-home kit they purchase at the grocery store. But he's smart and decides to do some data gathering with a TBYT before he spends a lot of money and time getting set up to deliver this service.

All he has to do is advertise the service to his existing patients. He does this the same way he would normally advertise to them, whether that's through posters in the waiting room or a pop-up box on his website. And his receptionist records all the people who show an interest. Not how many people "say" they are interested, but how many "actually" book an appointment (even though the real appointments aren't available quite yet). She may also take note of how many teeth whitening brochures people take, or how many times people call in asking about the service.

If there's enough interest, he moves ahead with the plan with a high chance of success. If there's not enough interest, he doesn't. And he's saved thousands of dollars he might otherwise have wasted on equipment and supplies.

Now it's your turn to practice the TBYT strategy:

Let's say our dentist is wondering whether he should start up an email newsletter. It's going to take time and money to send it out, and he's not sure anyone will even sign up for it. How could he use Test Before You Test to gather data and decide if this is worth his time?

You can use the practice sheet at the end of the chapter to write down your ideas.

GOOD TO KNOW

An Equation for Successful Email Marketing

Email marketing is an essential tool for just about any business, whether you sell online or offline. You want to make sure you have the right software and the right people behind you. Some experts say email marketing is dead, but it's just like any other tool. It's all in how you use email marketing. Here's a little equation for you:

Successful Email Marketing=
$$RC + RT + RL$$

Right Content + Right Timing + Right List

For more information, check out
www.FailureisObsolete.com/email-equation

HOW TO USE TEST BEFORE YOU TEST TO HIRE VIRTUAL EMPLOYEES

Another challenging part of running a business is hiring the right people to help you. I've found that if you're careful, hiring virtual employees can be a great way to thrive as a company. A virtual employee can work from anywhere in the world. They communicate with you online with the help of video conferencing services, email, and project management software.

Whether you hire a few virtual employees or run your entire company via the Internet, there are several major advantages.

>—You are not limited by the talent pool in your local area, so you can find the absolute best people for the job — even if they live halfway around the world.
>—Your company can run lean because you have little or no overhead invested in office space, equipment, and supplies. (You can also afford to pay more for your great talent.)
>—Your employees are happier because they can work in their own environment, on their own schedule.
>—You are happier because you can work in your own environment and on your own schedule (mostly).

There are some drawbacks, too.

>—You need to be very aware of time zones and what

hours are best for group meetings.
—You need to make sure there is no language or communication barrier.
—You need to invest in reliable computers, Internet access, and conferencing software.
—You need to have an excellent manager to keep on top of things. (You or someone you trust.) Tracking is more important than ever when you're a virtual company.

Most importantly, though, you must have a strategy for hiring the best people for the job. In addition to having top-notch skills in their field, they need to be self-motivated, great communicators, and good with deadlines.

Unfortunately, it seems these qualities are harder to find these days. Reliability is the number one skill you need in a virtual employee. There must be no doubt they will do what they say they'll do, when they say they'll do it. There's no one looking over his or her shoulder to make sure the work gets done.

You must require exceptional diligence in exchange for the awesome freedom of working from home (or the beach, or anywhere you want). The more common virtual companies become, the more diligent the workforce will become. At least, that's what I hope will happen.

Most of my current companies are at least partly virtual (if not completely). We've had great success hiring virtual employees over the years because we use the Test Before You Test strategy whenever we hire someone.

Think about the typical hiring process for a moment. You advertise the job opening and get a flood of resumes that all look more or less the same. Then you pick a few people to interview, talk to them about the job and about their qualifications. Finally, you narrow it down to a few finalists, interview them again, hire one of them and hope for the best. Sound familiar?

Resumes and interviews are a lot like surveys. They tell you a lot of "stuff" which may or may not turn out to be accurate in reality. No one is going to tell you straight out that they are sick a lot or have trouble getting assignments finished on time. You have to find that out the hard way.

What if we did a little data gathering in the right behavioral context *before* we even bothered doing an interview? What would that look like?

Let's pretend we're looking for some software coders. We've used oDesk.com with good luck before, so we'll use them again to find our applicants. We want to know whether they are skilled coders and can deliver on time in a real project situation. We don't even want to talk to someone who can't meet a deadline. So, we give them a real project to test them *before* we look at their resumes or credentials or interviewing them.

> **Audience:** ODesk users in the programming and coding category.
> **Action:** complete a project correctly and on time.
>
> **TBYT scenario:** Set up a live (paid) coding project with a tight deadline and see who passes the test. If they pass the small test, invite them to a larger (paid) project and see if they repeat the desired behavior. If they do, then start the interview process or what-

ever step comes next for you. It's worth paying a little money up front to save weeks of wasted time and energy (and money) later.

By running this TBYT scenario we are saving all the time and expense of going through a lengthy interviewing, hiring, and training process only to find the person doesn't really fit. We are proving the behavior we want to see before we even bother advertising the job opening.

If you have people in mind for the position, you can simply send them an invitation to view the job on ODesk. You are allowed to "hire" (test) as many people as you want for the job. It's a great way to narrow down the prospects in a hurry.

ODesk is handy for virtual hiring because they take care of much of the administrative hassle of bidding out a real project. But you can run the same kind of TBYT for hiring in-house employees using similar techniques.

For example, a lawyer I know was trying to hire a marketing assistant and getting nowhere with the usual routine. People would blow off the interview, or completely fail the short quiz he gave them. He was spending a ton of time and energy dealing with completely unqualified candidates.

So he decided to screen people before he spoke with them by testing them. He set up a web page that listed several tasks they had to complete in order to qualify for an interview. Each of these tasks was designed to prove that the candidate could perform certain tasks he needed the employee to do. And there was a time limit. He had never heard of Test Before You Test, but that's exactly what he was doing. Here's how it would have looked if we mapped it out on purpose.

Audience: Applicants from LinkedIn and Career-Builder.com
Action: Make and upload YouTube videos; write copy and post blogs
TBYT scenario: Ask all applicants to make a video application, post it on YouTube and then embed it into a special hiring blog as a post.

To see whether an applicant could perform the required tasks on time, he advertised the position and then told all interested parties to go to a certain web page to find out how to apply. To apply for the job, they had to first send him an email stating they were applying (that set a start time) and then make a video of why they should be hired. Then they had to upload it to YouTube (which proved they could make and upload videos) and then embed it in a blog post (which showed they knew how to use blogs).

The result? He had lots of people who applied, but never followed through with the directions. So, he didn't waste his time even talking to them. But he did have two people follow through brilliantly, and he had a great new assistant within days.

FIG 3.4: Finding good help can be extremely time consuming. Using a TBYT scenario to make applicants disqualify themselves means you only talk to the handful of truly qualified applicants. Make them perform tasks similar to ones they would do everyday on the job. If they can't do them for the application, you don't need to waste time interviewing them."

👍 GOOD TO KNOW

Tools For Running a Virtual Company

Running a virtual company can be a great experience for you and your employees. Everyone gets to work (mostly) on his or her own schedule, and in his or her own home. No commutes, no office gossip, and they can work in their PJs, if they want to. But you definitely need to invest in some tools to the work and communication flowing.

My web development company ClickCore has over a dozen team members and is 100% virtual. Everyone lives in a different state or country and works mostly from his or her home offices.

Here are some of the most important tools I've found for running a virtual company.

Computers:
This should go without saying, but everyone on your team needs a reliable computer, and preferably a backup. Ideally, they should all run on the same platform and have the same versions of any software you use regularly. This way everyone can share documents easily, without annoying hiccups.

Reliable Internet access:

Again, this should be a no-brainer. Unless you all live in the same city and can hold regular in-person meetings, you're going to need reliable Internet access to take care of business efficiently. If members of your team live in areas with spotty access, you should invest in a mobile backup source. The last thing you want is unexpected delays due to a thunderstorm or random outage.

FIG 3.5: My web development company, ClickCore, is 100% virtual. Over a dozen employees located all over the globe work in their own environments. Finding the right people can be a challenge, but TBYT can help.

 For more information, check out
www.FailureisObsolete.com/virtual-company

USING WEBSITES TO TEST BEFORE YOU TEST

A website is a powerful tool at your disposal for testing before you test. If you're testing ideas using flyers or newspaper ads or other offline methods, it can take a long time and more money than if you just whipped up a quick web page or online form. I know, that's easy for me to say. But what if you haven't been building websites all your life?

FIG 3.6: Testing with websites is so easy — it's like magic! It only takes an hour or so to build what you need using easy web builders like WordPress, Unbounce, and Infusionsoft.

You don't have to be some fancy-pants coder or graphic design ninja to use this tool. If you can make a blog post or send an email, you can use the most simple of web builders to do your data gathering for you. If you don't know how to make a blog post, or use a basic blog editor, what are you waiting for? It's simple to learn and will free you from the tyranny of waiting for other people to update your web pages.

There are a variety of great programs you can use to build simple websites and landing pages. Here are a few of my favorites:

- Unbounce (www.unbounce.com)
- Optimize Press (www.optimizepress.com)
- WordPress (www.wordpress.org)

For simple to use opt-in forms and email marketing, you can try these options:

- Infusionsoft (www.infusionsoft.com)
- Aweber (www.aweber.com)
- Constant Contact (www.constantcontact.com)

I👍 GOOD TO KNOW

How Non-Profits Can Benefit From the Test Before You Test Strategy, Too.

TBYT isn't just for business. Non-profits, charities, and other organizations can use this strategy, as well. You can test for the following: which appeals lead to more donations; which press releases get more media attention; which email campaigns get the most response; which social media posts get the most engagement. The list goes on and on.

Will anyone show up to a community garden planting? And will they continue to show interest in the project throughout the growing season?

Run a TBYT to find out if there's an interest in gardening by posting a flyer with a garden plotted out. Ask people to put their names on a plot on the map. Or hold an informational seminar on gardening at another community event that's already planned and see how many people show up.

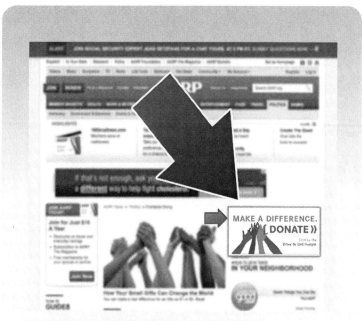

Fig 3.7 Test Before You Test is a good strategy for non-profit organizations that need to guard their hard-earned donations carefully. It can help bring in more donations, as well.

Any time you have a high-stakes decision to make, see if you can build a lower-risk TBYT scenario to test it first. Just remember the parameters:
Same Audience + Same Behavior =
Same Behavioral Context.

For more information, check out
www.FailureisObsolete.com/non-profit

Here are nine ways to test an audience using websites:

1. Landing pages — send traffic from your usual source (email, social media sites, banner ads, etc.) to a dedicated landing page that tests the behavior you're looking for. It could be testing interest in a new product or service. It could be testing whether people prefer to click a link or pick up the phone to get more information. Building one web page is much cheaper and faster than creating an entire marketing campaign for a project you don't know will succeed.

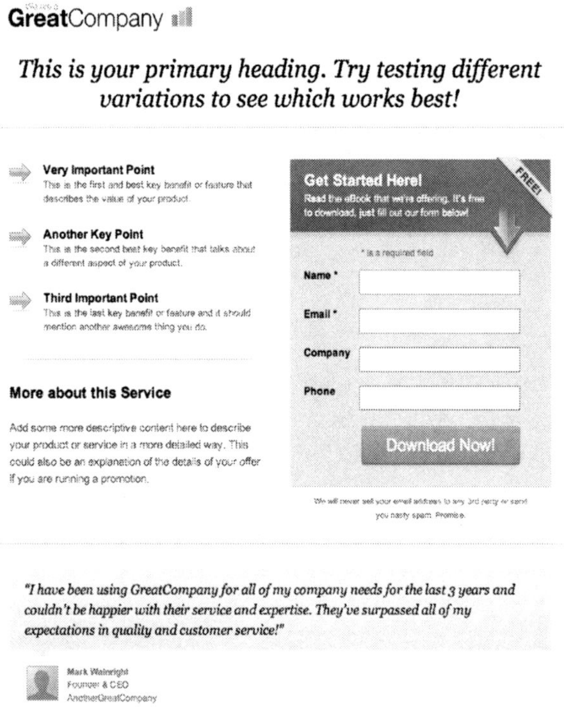

GreatCompany

This is your primary heading. Try testing different variations to see which works best!

Very Important Point
This is the first and best key benefit or feature that describes the value of your product.

Another Key Point
This is the second best key benefit that talks about a different aspect of your product.

Third Important Point
This is the last key benefit or feature and it should mention another awesome thing you do.

More about this Service

Add some more descriptive content here to describe your product or service in a more detailed way. This could also be an explanation of the details of your offer if you are running a promotion.

Get Started Here!
Read the eBook that we're offering. It's free to download, just fill out our form below!

FREE!

* is a required field

Name *

Email *

Company

Phone

Download Now!

We will never sell your email address to any 3rd party or send you nasty spam. Promise.

"I have been using GreatCompany for all of my company needs for the last 3 years and couldn't be happier with their service and expertise. They've surpassed all of my expectations in quality and customer service!"

Mark Wainright
Founder & CEO
AnotherGreatCompany

Fig 3.8a Building one web page and running a TBYT for orders, phone calls, clicked links, etc. is so much faster and cheaper than creating an entire marketing campaign for a project you aren't sure will succeed. (Screenshot from unbounce - an easy web-building platform. Find out more at www.FailureisObsolete.com/unbounce.)

2. Sign up forms — putting a form on your existing website is another way to test interest in a new idea. It takes about ten minutes to set up a web form and post it on your existing site. Then you just sit back and see if anyone signs up.

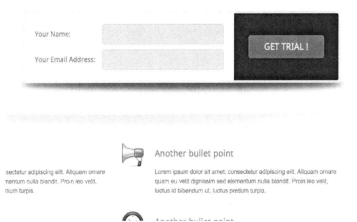

Fig 3.8b Web forms can be as short as "name and email" or they can capture more detailed information like company, website, phone number, etc. The shorter the form, the more likely people are to fill it out. If you want lots of information, try using multi-step forms. Get their name and email first, then ask for other information on a separate screen.

3. Blog comments — Wondering if you should bother setting up social media campaigns to engage your customers? Try encouraging comments on your blog posts first. If you get lots of comments on a particular topic, that might be a good sign they will engage in conversation on Facebook or Twitter as well. Social media is all about engagement, getting people talking about you or your business. So use your existing communication channels to test engagement before you go through all the time and effort of setting up and maintaining social media.

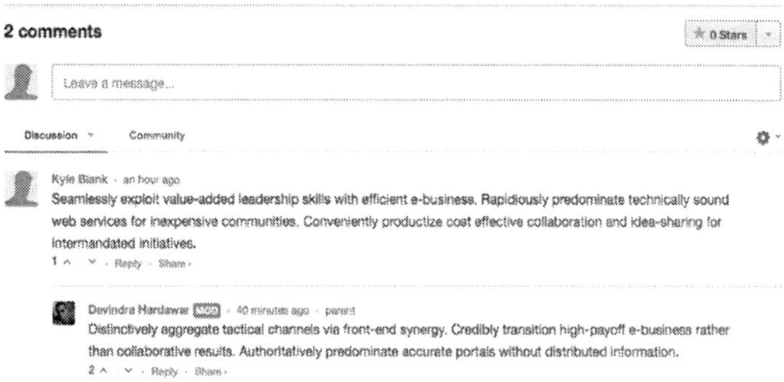

Fig 3.8c Social media campaigns can take up a lot of time and energy. Before you launch headlong into Facebook, Twitter, or any other social platform, try engaging people on your blog first. If people enjoy commenting, and engagement comes easily, then social media could be a good way to expand your network. (Screenshot from DISQUS)

4. Shopping cart upsell and cross-sell — Another way to test interest in a new offer is to try upselling or cross-selling in your shopping cart or order forms. Will people who order dog toys from you also order dog food? Present the option as an addition to the product being purchased (as long as it makes sense in context). Remember, you don't need to actually sell the dog food just yet. You're just looking to see if anyone expresses interest.

Fig 2.8d Upselling on a "thank you" page is a great way to test a product idea before you create it. Just count how many actual orders are placed. (Screenshot from Amazon.com)

5. Someone else's website — You don't have a website and aren't sure you want to build one? Try utilizing someone else's site to see if you get interest in your offerings. Create a joint venture arrangement to test whether that person can sell your products for you (with compensation of some kind).

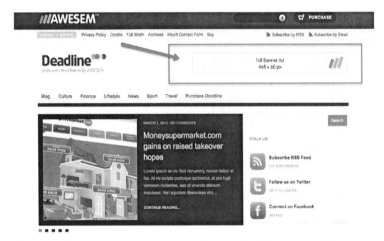

Fig 3.8e Joint venture partners can be a valuable resource for testing ideas. Find someone with a large audience of people like the ones you want to sell to. Determine if that partner will sell your products (for a commission) to test how well the audience responds.

6. Blog posts — Blog posts can be a great way to test ideas with your audience. Test their reactions. Do they like or dislike your idea? What are their comments? It's also a great way to test headlines for emails or sales pages and advertising. Which headlines get the most readers? Which posts wind up being shared across the Internet?

Fig 3.8f You can run a TBYT by simply writing a blog post and asking for comments. How well does your audience react to the idea? You never know, they may give you some valuable input you hadn't thought of before.

7. Graphics and images — Wondering if some new packaging or branding will help sell more products? Test it online first with your product images before you go out and have your entire line reworked. How do people react? Do they even notice? Do you get more orders using the old branding or the new?

Fig 3.8g Simply changing graphics or branding and tracking the reactions of your prospects and customers can be an eye-opening TBYT. Did sales go up or down?

8. Banner ads — Putting advertising on your own or someone else's website is a quick way to determine interest. All you do is count the clicks. Remember you need to have decent traffic and the same audience for this to work. Putting an ad for dog food on a website for model trains doesn't make sense.

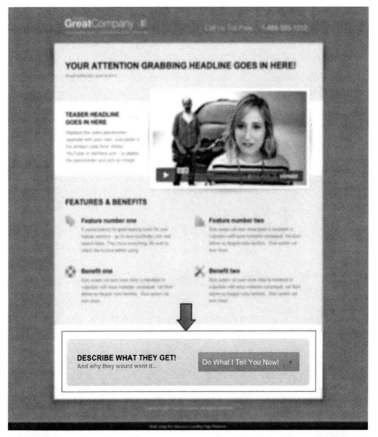

Fig 3.8h Put a banner ad on someone else's high-traffic website and track the clicks. This can be a good indication of interest. Just be sure to use a website with the same audience as yours. (Screenshot from Unbounce - an easy web building platform. Find out more at www.FailureisObsolete.com/unbounce.)

9. Pay Per Click ads — This one is my favorite, but it's a bit technical to go into here. Basically, you're using quick, cheap advertising to see what people will respond to. Then you use that data to formulate your new marketing campaigns.

We'll spend some time on this special technique in the next chapter. (So keep reading!)

Fig 3.8i There's a whole technique to using pay-per-click advertising as a TBYT method. Be sure to check out the detailed explanation in the next chapter.

Overall, most business decisions can be tested to assure the best path to success. There are so many unknowns when you're an entrepreneur. But you can narrow down the choices to the ones with the best chance for success by simply running a TBYT scenario as often as possible. Whenever I'm faced with a choice, my first thought is always *how could I test this idea to get the best possible outcome with the lowest time and cost investment.*

I👍 GOOD TO KNOW

How To Use TBYT To Test Live Events.

Here's another way to use TBYT in your business using MeetUp.com
We have a client who has a very large membership list. They are a global organization with tens of thousands of people, all using online educational materials to improve their skills in their chosen careers. But our client was missing a huge benefit to their organization — a networking component. After all, being able to meet and interact with thousands of your peers around the world is a pretty big benefit. People might buy a membership for that aspect alone.

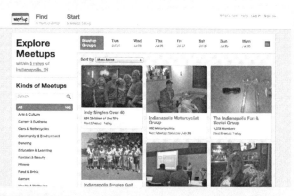

Fig 3.9a Meetup.com is a social media website where people can organize and find groups in their interest areas.

We asked them if they had ever done any live events where members could get together, meet each other, and share ideas. They admitted they hadn't thought of that and then immediately started thinking of all the hard work (and money) it would entail. A live event is always a big risk the first time out.

So we suggested they run a TBYT of sorts. Instead of just creating some huge expensive extravaganza and hoping it would succeed, they would test their membership's true interest in getting together in person. All they would have to do is set up an account on MeetUp.com and let their members know they could plan small meetups with other members in their own area.

Fig 3.9b When people in a certain group will voluntarily meet up for coffee in their local area, there's a good chance they'll also attend a more formal live event.

For more information, check out
www.FailureisObsolete.com/meetup

THINGS TO REMEMBER

GOALS & ACTIONABLES

TBYT PRACTICE SHEET

Audience:

_____

_____

_____

Action:

_____

_____

_____

_____

Test:

_____

_____

_____

_____

_____

_____

_____

_____

4. CONVERSION RATE OPTIMIZATION (CRO)

How to use the Test Before You Test strategy to help your website be more effective, and more profitable.

Anyone with an online presence for their business can benefit from testing their websites. Large companies like Amazon and Google are constantly testing which versions of a page will bring in more money, get more signups, and such. The percentage of viewers that actually convert by taking a certain action is called a conversion rate. And the science of continually tweaking a web page, site, or other marketing campaign for higher and higher conversion is called conversion rate optimization (or CRO for short).

This chapter will cover the basic concepts of conversion rate optimization first, and then I'll show you how you can use the same techniques my CRO company uses to get great results using the Test Before You Test strategy.

NOTE: If you already know what CRO is and how to use split-testing to improve your web pages, you can probably skip this intro section. But be sure to read the rest of the chapter with examples of real Test Before You Test (TBYT) scenarios I've used for successful data gathering and awesome results.

Conversion Rate Optimization Basics

When a visitor stumbles across your website, what happens?

> — Do they browse around for a while?
> — Do they buy something?
> — Do they signup for your newsletter?
> — Do they just click the back button on their browser without even reading your site?

More importantly, what do you want them to do? What is the goal?

Every page on your website should have a goal, even if that goal is to click through to the next page, or the next article. The percentage of people who complete the action you want them to take is generally called a conversion rate.

You usually want the visitor to do several things; therefore, I will divide this term up into two types — "Micro Conversion Rate" and "Bottom Line Conversion Rate".

For example, if 100 people come to your web page advertising sailboats and 10 people buy from that page, you have a 10% Bottom Line Conversion Rate. (That's pretty awesome for a high-ticket item like a boat!) But what if only one person buys? Then you have a 1% conversion rate. That rate might be okay, but you'd like to do better. So, you make some changes here and there. Maybe you changed the pictures on the page, or made the order button bigger, or improved your descriptions a bit. And if two people buy, you now have a 2% conversion rate.

You just doubled your income without paying any more for advertising or traffic generation. Pretty sweet.

Of course, it takes lots of steps to get someone to buy a boat online. They need to find the boat they want on your site, navigate through your shopping cart, make the payment or set up a credit arrangement, etc.

Each of these micro steps has its own conversion rate — a micro conversion rate. If you tweak your shopping cart to get twice as many people completing the process, you've doubled your micro conversion rate. The cool thing here is that a small improvement to one micro step can mean huge improvements in your Bottom Line Conversion Rate.

Of course, it works in reverse, too. If your tweaks result in a smaller micro-conversion rate, you could be looking at much lower bottom line revenues. This is why testing and tracking are so important, and why businesses hire companies like mine to handle it for them.

This is conversion rate optimization in a nutshell, and it can get pretty addictive. Every little tweak can help you earn exponentially more money, or it can hurt you just as badly. That's why it's important not to go about CRO willy-nilly, guessing at what changes might improve your conversion rates. That's trial and error and can be really bad for business if you get it wrong, especially if you're not tracking measurable results.

Guessing is just a waste of time, energy, and potentially big money. After all, if you were making $1,000 or more a day and you make a change that hurts you rather than helps, you could lose a lot of money before you figured out what was happening. It's a pretty big risk for a guess. Fortunately, split testing can provide a measure of safety around what you're changing. Split testing lowers your risk by telling you exactly which version (the old or the new) is getting more conversions.

Here's how split testing works:
You decide to make a change to a web page, but rather than just making the change and hoping for the best (trial and error) you decide to test whether the new version really does better than the original version. So you create the modified page and enter both pages into a special piece of split testing software. That software automatically divides your traffic in half. One-half goes to the original page, and the other half goes to the new page. (Your visitors don't know this is happening, it's secret.) Then the software measures what percentage of people convert on each page. The conversion might be anything — clicking a link, filling out a form, or making a purchase.

It's like a race. Sometimes the pages are neck and neck for a long time. Sometimes there's an early front-runner that proves to be the loser in the end. But most of the time the software will show you a clear conversion winner as long as you leave the test running long enough. That becomes your new "control" page (no matter which version it is). And then you start all over again, testing a different "new version" of the page against the control.

Here's the problem with most split testing:
How in the world do you know what changes to make? Most people (even most experts) guess randomly and hope for the best.

They congratulate themselves for being "testers" who are always trying to improve. Maybe they even hire a CRO company to provide insight into what they should test. But unless that company is using data-gathering tests first, it's more risky than it has to be, and it can wind up costing more money in the long run.

In this case, the CRO company is basically just guessing, too. They will have data from past clients, which can help them make better guesses than you could make on your own — maybe — but it's still guessing.

So most business owners and CRO experts play the game like this:

1) Spend time (and money) conducting surveys, and gathering the best existing data they can find using demographics and other methods.
2) Guess at a change that might improve conversions.
3) Implement the guess.
4) Split test the guess and hope for quick data, then go with the "winner" version.
5) Wash, rinse, and repeat.

The problem here is that it can take weeks or months to get a clear winner in a split test, and you could lose a LOT of money during that test. Most of the money wasted is needlessly spent building out the test variations.

Here's one way my CRO company, ConversionCore, does things differently and partly why our success rate is much higher than most in our industry:

1) Design a low-risk data-gathering TBYT scenario around a certain change you want to make.
2) Split test the scenario to determine the *actual behavior* of your visitors regarding the change.
3) Use the results to design the best variation to be tested.

4) Implement a "real" split test based on the "pre-tested" conclusion.
5) Wash, rinse, and repeat.
6) Watch the extra moolah come rolling in.

When we work for conversion increases by testing before we test, not guessing, we get successful outcomes almost every time. Our success rates are often far higher than even the biggest companies in the CRO industry, and the TBYT strategy is a big reason why.

(We'll go into some real-world examples from my company in just a minute.)

Micro Conversions vs. Bottom Line Conversion Rate
So now you know you should be testing your web pages for conversion, and you shouldn't be guessing about what changes to make. But where do you start, especially if you have a huge website?

Every business owner is looking for a boost to his or her bottom line. The end result of almost every test is, "Did I make more money?" I call this the Bottom Line Conversion Rate. And it's a great way to measure success. However, every Bottom Line Conversion Rate is made up of lots and lots of smaller conversions. I call these micro conversions. The percentage of times those micro-conversions are successful is what I call the Micro Conversion Rate.

After all, a conversion is just a decision. And a visitor to your website needs to make lots and lots of tiny decisions before they decide to buy something from you. The cool thing about micro conversions is that one little tweak to a smaller process can have a huge impact on your Bottom Line Conversion Rate.

Please note that while not every website has the goal of making money, every site does have a goal. The techniques I'm about to show you apply to all your online goals — whether you want people to buy, or sign up for your mailing list, volunteer their time, or donate their old cars to your charity. Each of those goals requires conversions. So even though I'm using business examples, the techniques are equally valid for nonprofits and other organizations.

I recommend starting your conversion testing on the product, service, or goal that's going to give you the most bang for your buck — the highest return on investment (ROI.) That's probably the thing you sell that provides the highest profit margin or your most popular product.

When I consult with clients, we usually start by looking at their funnel leading up to the sale of that particular product. Your funnel is just the series of steps a visitor takes to get to your conversion goal. Most people think of having one funnel — their sales funnel. The steps are something like "prospect, lead, nurture, sale" or more often just "prospect, sale." These basic sales funnels are pretty short-sighted and can lose lots of potentially great customers. They're more like sieves than funnels, leaking profit all over the place.

But when you think about micro conversions as their own little funnels, you can start to make some real progress on improving your Bottom Line Conversion Rates.

👍 GOOD TO KNOW

What Is a Click Through Rate (CTR) and How Can It Help You?

The "Click Through Rate" (CTR) is the number of times people click on a web page, link, or an ad compared to the number of people who saw that page, link, or ad. If 100 people see your ad for vitamin supplements, and 10 people click the ad, you have a 10% click through rate. In other words, 10% of people "clicked through" to go to the next step (whether that's making a purchase or just finding out more information).

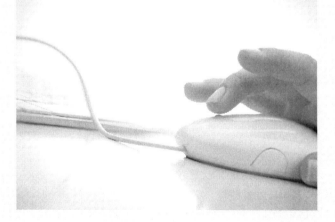

Every time a person clicks a link or a button, they are making a decision. That decision represents a "micro conversion point." Often that click is the first conversion point in a sales process, so it's a very important one. The more often people click on your links and buttons, the more interested they may be in what you have to offer and the more likely they'll keep on clicking .

Unless your CTR is 100% all the time, there's always more optimizing you can do, improvements you can make, and split tests you can run.

3 Tips To Improve CTR on a web page:

1. Include clickable elements in several places on the page.

2. Make sure it is clear the element is meant to be clicked on (underlined links, or obviously shaped buttons).

3. Include benefit-driven text on the clickable element.

 For more information, check out www.FailureisObsolete.com/click-through-rate

HERE'S A GREAT PLACE TO START: THE DOUBLE FUNNEL TECHNIQUE

This is the place I usually start with my clients — the double funnel technique. It almost always leads to major increases in conversions, and it's easy to implement.

Say you have a sales page, and you have a traffic stream leading to the page. If they buy, you get them. If they don't buy, they're gone. That's an extremely small funnel. Are most people going to be ready to buy right away? Probably not, especially if they've never heard of you.

Could you possibly convince them to convert later on through email or direct mail? Maybe. But you'll never get the chance to try without having a second funnel in place *before* your sales funnel.

In the double funnel technique, we add a layer before the sales funnel. This first layer contains a way for visitors to opt-in to your mailing list. That just means visitors can give you their contact information in return for more education about something they're interested in.

We almost always add a free, or nearly free, incentive for visitors to give you their information: a free report or white paper download; a video series; a tutorial — whatever will give them more education on the subject and encourage them to buy.

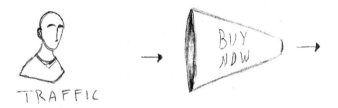

FIG 4.1: Before: Most sales funnels are extremely short, just taking traffic and converting to sales. This is difficult and wastes time on nonqualified leads.

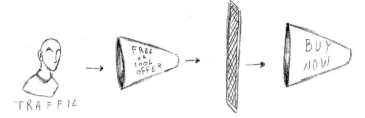

FIG 4.2: After: In the double funnel technique, you attract traffic through a lead-generation funnel with a free or nearly-free offer, capture their contact information, screen out the unqualified leads and send the hot ones through the sales funnel.

The basic idea is you're adding a micro conversion layer to your process in order to increase your Bottom Line Conversion Rate. The goal is to get contact information from your visitors before they leave your site so you can continue to market to them over time. Unless your prospect is 100% sold when they land on your website, chances are they will need tips, examples, or even small samples of your wares to help persuade them to buy.

Very few people will come to your site and buy on the spot. They need time to think. Maybe they need some questions answered. Maybe they need to wait until pay-day. Maybe they need to wait until their kids' nap time so they can browse undisturbed. It doesn't matter the reason — once a visitor leaves your site, they will probably never come back, even if they intended to. So you put this lead funnel in place to collect their information as soon as possible. Then if they get distracted and click away, it's okay. You'll be in touch with them later.

Generally speaking, the more expensive the items you're selling are, the more important it is to have a lead-gathering double funnel in place. It takes longer to decide to spend more money. There are more questions that need to be answered. Perhaps a phone call is necessary to close the sale. This extra funnel takes less than an hour to put into action, and it can exponentially increase your sales. Low risk, high reward. Pretty sweet, right?

Here's an example:
Let's say you're selling a subscription to the Chocolate of the Month Club online. You set up a sales page for it with a big "Buy Now" button. Visitors will either buy or they won't. What happens to the people who come to the site and then leave? How many will come back? Almost none - ever. So, how can you capture them to keep them in the funnel?

There are lots of ways to solve this problem, here's one idea: You could add a step where they sign up to get a free sample mailed to them. (Who doesn't like free chocolate?) People not ready to buy now aren't risking much by having you send a free sample. All they're doing is giving you their mailing address and maybe an email. But that information is gold for conversion purposes. You can now use new strategies like email marketing, and direct mail to encourage them to buy later. Maybe you even convince them to buy subscriptions as gifts for friends and family.

Overall, you're closing more sales; your Bottom Line Conversion Rate increases dramatically, and you've increased the ROI on your existing advertising. All by simply putting up a web form and sending a free sample in the mail. One micro conversion tweak did all that.

When you're looking for a place to start optimizing, look at your marketing and sales funnels. Do you have a lead generating opt-in funnel? If not, make one! Get help if you need to.

Then start looking at all the micro conversion points inside your website. Where can you make small changes that will reap big rewards?

- Traffic streams
- Lead generation
- Email marketing sequences
- Sales pages
- Product descriptions
- Shopping cart
- Success pages
- Upsell pages
- Referral sequences
- Direct mail
- Pay-per-click ads

There are micro conversion points in all these areas you can improve upon.

— Could you get better pictures or copy?
— Do your readers get lost in too much text?
— Is your signup button buried at the bottom of the page?
— Does your header take up too much space?

When you apply smart changes and confirm the results with split testing, you're well on your way.

Now let's look at how you can go even further by using Test Before You Test strategies for conversion.

HOW TO USE TEST BEFORE YOU TEST FOR CONVERSION RATE OPTIMIZATION ON YOUR WEBSITE.

NOTE: With my company ConversionCore, I've been fortunate to work with amazing people involved in small businesses right on up to Fortune 500 companies. Part of the beauty of having a CRO expert on your side is that your competition never knows how or why you are suddenly growing so fast. I like to keep my clients confidential in order to keep their competitors guessing about why their conversions are so high. So, the examples I list here may or may not be real clients, the tests are real, but the identities are changed to protect the innocent. (Thank you *Dragnet!*)

Remember the premise of Test Before You Test is to test very small, low-risk things first to give you an idea of actual market behavior before you test the higher-risk things. Test one is for data-gathering purposes to help you make a better decision for the "real" test. The goal, of course, is to gain confidence that your test will be successful before you start. Using this method allows you to get bigger conversion increases, more often, because you start with a higher probability of success.

👍 GOOD TO KNOW

Tools For Conversion Rate Optimization

The more data you have about visitor behavior on your website, the better you'll become at designing TBYT and split test scenarios. After all, you don't want to just guess what changes will bring higher conversions — you want to *know* with a fair degree of certainty.

Analytics tools can go a long way toward showing you what's happening when visitors come to your site. Do they browse around? Do they go straight to the item they want and buy it? Are they skipping over the most important elements? Or do they get confused and just leave?

There are tools that can give you heat maps of where people focus most. They can show you eye-tracking maps of the path a visitor's eye actually follows on a certain page. They can even show you a video of mouse clicks and browsing patterns. It's pretty amazing. Most of these types of tools have free trials. So, even if you don't plan to spend your days analyzing data, it's good to get a general feel for how people use your site.

For a list of my favorite analytics tools, check out the webpage below.

Fig 4.3: Heat maps show you exactly where your visitors' attention is focused on your webpage. This valuable information allows you to adjust the graphic design to improve conversions.

For more information, check out
www.FailureisObsolete.com/conversion-tools

Let's look at some actual examples of how my company uses TBYT scenarios to improve conversions for our clients.

Example #1: Latin lovers?

A few years ago, we were working with a large e-commerce website. (I can't divulge the exact company, but for our purposes here let's say it was Amazon.com.)

They were considering building a Spanish language and Latin culture website as their next big project with the goal being to raise conversions among their Spanish-speaking visitors.

Why would they decide to do something like this? The idea didn't come out of the blue. They had survey data that said Spanish-speaking people were a large percentage of their customer base.

The red-flag keyword to me was "customer." I explained to them that they may not want to tailor their site to "customers" (who have already purchased) but to "prospects." I felt testing the prospects' behavior might yield more telling data.

 It sounded like a good idea. After all, there are lots of Spanish-speaking visitors on their site. But it was a very high-risk proposition. They would have to spend hundreds of thousands of dollars to build the new site, and there was no guarantee that it would positively affect conversions. ($100,000 to them might be $1,000 to you. Everyone's risk tolerance and marketing budget is unique.)

Their original plan was to spend the money, build the site, and then test it for conversions. We recommended strongly that they run a data-gathering Test Before You Test scenario first to see if it was worth spending the money at all. Our goal was to minimize the possibility of failure to almost zero. If testing is "failing as fast as you can" (as some experts put it), our strategy prevents the necessity to fail at all.

We wanted to discover two things: (1) whether they should build a site all in Spanish, and (2) whether they should add a "Latin Products" section with clickable links on their current English site. So we designed a simple TBYT scenario to get the answer quickly and very inexpensively.

Audience: Existing visitors to the website

Action: Click on a link or button in Spanish

TBYT scenario: We had them add a simple button in a prominent space across the website that simply said "En Espanol." Then we counted how many people clicked. (When they clicked, they were greeted with a friendly "coming soon" page.)

Notice we didn't *ask* them if they would use a Spanish site. That would be using the survey method, which may or may not provide accurate results. We were looking for actual behavior. All we wanted to know was whether it was worth building out a Spanish version of the site and split testing that version for conversion increases later on. We got our answer in short order.

It turned out it was more than worth their money to make the change. In this case, it was absolutely necessary! And because we found out so quickly, they were making revenue off the new Spanish site much faster than if they had just built it over time and hoped for the best. They knew it would be a success, so they were motivated to move forward quickly. They now had great confidence that the investment was going to create a high return. In their situation, this small piece of valuable data led to better than anticipated results.

The revenue potential of the market was much larger than originally thought. So they ended up putting more resources into the project than originally planned. They increased the priority and budget for the entire site, and we wound up creating a special team dedicated to helping them implement the project.

The total cost to run this test, including building and testing, was less than $2,000 and two days of online testing time. This company saved six months and hundreds of thousands of dollars in lost revenue just by using the Test Before You Test strategy.

Large companies like Amazon benefit from the TBYT strategy because a tiny 2% lift in response can be worth millions. They know the value of one successful tweak. But if you're a smaller company, you can benefit even more by using TBYT to avoid costly mistakes caused by guessing or trial and error.

Example #2: Mobile demand.
Here's an example from our own testing for my software company, AutomationCore. We develop useful business applications, many of which tie in with the popular business software, Infusionsoft. (Check out www.FailureisObsolete.com/Infusionsoft for more information on Infusionsoft.) A few people mentioned they would love to have a mobile version of one of our apps because their sales force

was out in the field a lot. They needed to have access to Infusionsoft on their phones.

We had to decide if it was worth the time and money to develop a whole mobile platform for this application. It would have been very expensive to just create it and hope people wanted it enough to buy. So, we designed a TBYT to help us see how much actual interest there was.

All we did was add a button at the bottom of our home page and in a few other places in our marketing that said "Mobile App" and waited to see how many people clicked that link. We also tracked how many people asked us about a mobile app in person or over the phone.

The answer surprised us. It told us we needed to make mobile a real priority and quickly! Not only was it faster and easier than sending out a survey, but it also gave us more accurate results (and a list of people who wanted to buy once it was ready).

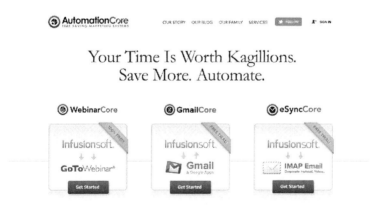

FIG 4.4: All we had to do to run this TBYT was add a small link titled "Mobile App" to the bottom of the screen. It proved to be very worth our while to develop this app, based on the response we received. So I made the investment with full confidence.

Example #3: Larger text across the board.

Here's an example from a much smaller company. Years ago, I worked with an online merchant with a target audience of people over the age of 55. We wondered if having larger text on the website would improve conversions, since eyesight tends to decline with age. It would have cost thousands of dollars to change the whole site for this large company, so we designed a TBYT to figure out if it was a worthwhile investment.

We enlarged the text size in a common email campaign and on a couple of major landing pages. The goal was to see if the new text size did indeed affect conversion rates by having more people than usual open the email and click on the links inside and on the landing pages.

After a month we knew it was worth it to increase text size everywhere, not just the website. If we had only done the TBYT on the landing pages, the client might have missed out on a major opportunity for more revenue through their email list. It made sense to us because if text size mattered on the website, it would also matter on any materials read on a screen — including email, banner advertising, web forms, and text messages.

Because we used a TBYT scenario, it was almost a sure thing that the changes would produce more revenue and the investment would be worth it.

We knew we had a great TBYT because it was low risk, easy to do, and attainable with minimal extra work. It minimized loss and maximized the information gathered.

Example #4: Sometimes the tests prove us wrong.
Of course, the tests don't always tell us to move forward
with an idea. Sometimes they prove our assumptions
wrong and help us prevent costly mistakes. One example
of this comes from a website that sells high-end luxury
products that cost more than $1,000.

The owner was spending hundreds of thousands of dollars
on Google advertising, and each sale required a high level
of education to get people to buy. (In other words, it took a
lot of text to persuade people to open their wallets for this
product.)

He came to us for help getting more phone calls from the
website to their sales representatives because that's where
the most sales came from. Or so he thought.

I asked him what percentage of online sales did NOT come
from a phone call first. He replied "almost none." It was his
belief that every person who bought online had first called
in and spoken to someone live. In this scenario, it made
sense to try to encourage people to call in as soon as possible. The sooner they called, the more likely they would
buy. But being who I am, I was naturally cautious. I didn't
want to hurt his bottom line revenues by changing things
at random (guessing).

So I decided to run a TBYT scenario to test his assumptions about the online sales.

I designed a test to easily discover how many of the website customers had talked to a team member by phone. At
a glance, I didn't have any reason to suspect the owner was
wrong. But in order to maintain the likelihood of success, I
wanted to test those assumptions, just to be sure. (This was

in his first month of working with us, by the way. He was skeptical, I'll admit. But he went along with it.)

He was unwilling to ask customers directly, but he was willing to put an additional question on the order form. So that's what we did. We added one line that said "Did you speak with a representative before making this purchase? Yes/No."

Of course, there's room for a margin of error because we weren't testing actual behavior, we were asking a question (basically taking a survey). But it was a creative solution that gave us the data we needed.

Within three weeks we found out that over 90% of people who ordered online never spoke to anyone on the phone! And online sales account for half their total revenue.

That's huge. If we had done what they requested and used strategies to get people calling in sooner, they may have lost a lot of money. At best, they might have broken even. It was definitely NOT worth the six months and thousands of dollars in consulting fees he was planning to spend with us.

When he saw this data, he was in shock. He had absolutely no idea that this was the case. And he instantly understood the value of what we do as conversion rate optimization experts and why the TBYT strategy is so amazing. Knowing his business model combined with experience from past customers with similar situations, I can tell you he saved hundreds of thousands of dollars and a year of his life focusing on the wrong thing.

It's very likely this was the reason why the company had been unexplainably shrinking over the previous five years. This was the very first test we designed for him. It was implemented in one day, for less than $100.

Pretty awesome results.

👍 GOOD TO KNOW

Conversion Rate Optimization
Split-Testing Tools For Your Website

It's all fine and dandy to say you want to test which version of a web page gets the most orders, but how exactly do you do that? You do it with something called split-testing software.

The process goes something like this:

1. Create two (or more) versions of a web page.
2. Input both URLs (web addresses) into the software.
3. The software automatically splits your traffic between the two pages and keeps track of which one accomplishes the goal more efficiently.
4. When you have a clear winner, you make that page your new "control" page. Then you repeat the process with a new challenger page.

Large companies like Google and Amazon are constantly split testing their pages for better conversion. Unless your conversion rate is 100% of your visitor traffic, there's always room for improvement.

FIG 4.5: Split testing is a valuable tool for conversion rate optimization. It allows you to test two or more versions of a web page against each other to see which one does the best job of converting. The trick is to never be done spli testing. As soon as you have a winner, you test another idea out with another version of the page. This way you are constantly improving your conversion rates.

There are several split testing software companies you can go with. Some have more features than others; one is even completely free. For a list of our favorite split testing tools, check out the web page below.

For more information, check out
www.FailureisObsolete.com/split-testing

FACADE TESTING: USING PAY-PER-CLICK (PPC) ADVERTISING TO GET THE ANSWERS YOU NEED QUICKLY AND EASILY.

Getting the proper audience to Test Before You Test can sometimes be difficult, especially if your company is brand new. Maybe you don't have a mailing list, and barely any website or social media traffic. Maybe you don't even have a business yet, just an idea. If that's you, don't despair!

If you don't have your own environment to test in, you can test cheaply and quickly in the vast expansive reaches of pay-per-click advertising. You can reach any audiences you need easily with just a few clicks and a small budget.

According to the dictionary, a "facade" is an outward appearance that is maintained to conceal a less pleasant or incomplete reality. Movie sets are a good example. You see the facade of a building with a big sign that says "bank" on the screen and imagine the whole building is there. But in reality, there is only the front and enough of the sides to "look" real. It's deceptive, but sometimes necessary to make things cheaper or faster. Building a whole bank from scratch isn't necessary. It would take too long and cost too much. Besides, the director just needs to get the idea across.

You can do the same thing with websites by driving traffic to a facade site that looks realistic and has real information on it, but is actually only one or two quickie pages designed to test an idea.

My companies use facade testing frequently to transform complicated, risky decisions into simple, fast tests. (Why would we guess at the right choice and risk being wrong, when we can spend a day or a week testing and *know* which is the correct way to go?)

In this section, I'm going to show you some great ways to use TBYT with with pay-per-click advertising, also known as PPC or "paid search." But first, let's take a quick look at the different types of pay-per-click and why you may want to use both kinds for your testing.

Most people immediately think of Google AdWords when they hear PPC. These ads are found in the yellow band of "sponsored ads" that show up in your results whenever you search for something on Google. Advertisers pay to be in those search results. Every time someone clicks on the ad, Google gets paid a small fee (sometimes a large one).

Search engines like Google try to give you the best results as possible based on what you search. Pay-per-click advertising is basically bribing Google to put your result first. You pay them their bribe each time someone clicks your link.

AdWords is by far the largest and most common PPC platform out there, but the other search engines (Bing, Yahoo, etc.) have their own ad networks that work the same way. This is known as pay-per-click advertising.

FIG 4.6: Paid search or pay-per-click (PPC) reaches people who are actually searching for what you have to offer. Running tests using PPC can be a great way to research your market quickly and cheaply.

You are reaching people who are actually searching for something related to your products or services.

Another form of PPC includes social media advertising, some types of banner advertising, and content network advertising. The primary difference between these and paid search is that these ads just show up unannounced.

Facebook is a good example. The ads that show up on the side of your feed are PPC ads, but they are not related to any specific searches you performed. The network decides what ads to display based on lots of data collected about you and your friends and your demographics. They try to display the ads you'll be most interested in.

FIG 4.7: Facebook matches their ads to what they think you're most interested in. Sometimes they're right, and sometimes they're not. But testing people's reactions when they aren't actually looking for you can provide valuable data.

👍 GOOD TO KNOW

Using Facebook Advertising as a Test Before You Test Platform

Just like using Google AdWords, you can also use Facebook as your pay-per-click platform of choice for the TBYT strategy. The main difference is with AdWords, you are targeting people who are searching for certain keywords. Facebook ads target people interested in certain things, but who aren't actively searching for information. It's a different audience, so make sure you use the correct platform to match your desired audience.

Also just like AdWords, Facebook advertising can get expensive (and return poor results) unless you know what you're doing. I highly recommend reading *The Ultimate Guide to Facebook Advertising*, by Thomas Meloche and Perry Marshall. It will help you get better results for less money.

Perry Marshall, author of the #1 selling book on Google advertising, and Internet strategist, Thomas Meloche, lift the curtain to the 600 million potential customers on Facebook and show you how to reach them, convert them, and keep them as your fan, friend, and customer for life.

Introducing game-changing strategies, tools, and reports, Marshall and Meloche breakdown the magic of Facebook paid advertising and show you how to gain dramatically on your investment—in clicks, customers, and profits.

Covers critical updates including:

- Targeting by birthday, family status, and more
- Pinpointing who is seeing your ads
- Managing impressions to avoid ad fatigue
- Using Sponsored Story Ads
- Creating a Facebook business and identity

 For more information, check out
www.FailureisObsolete.com/Facebook

The important thing to remember here is that one type of PPC is displayed according to search, and another just shows up in front of you. That gives you two distinct audiences — searchers and non-searchers. When you're using TBYT together with PPC to gather information about an idea, it's important to think about which type of audience you want to reach. Or whether collecting data from both types might be worthwhile.

AdWords/Bing/Yahoo search ads = people searching for info (same as your current customers or mailing list).

Facebook/LinkedIn/Banner Ads = People not searching for info (same as a blind list).

I hope the examples on the following pages will make it clearer.

Example #1: TBYT for email subject lines.

Marketing experts have been predicting the death of email for years now. They complain that no one opens his emails or reads the content. Maybe it's not the reader that's the problem. Maybe they just have crappy subject lines.

If you don't grab the reader's attention with a great subject line, they will not bother to open or read the email. Having a professional copywriter do your writing for you can help, but even they don't hit it out of the park every time.

I had a client who had a potentially very profitable email campaign she wanted to send out to her large list. She knew what her open rates were normally, and wanted to improve that for this campaign by improving the subject line. Most experts would recommend she split test her list by sending half the people one subject line and the other half, another subject line. Then see which half produced better results for her.

That's all well and good, except she would be losing money on the people who didn't open the losing subject line. She wanted better odds. She wanted to minimize the risk and maximize the success rate of the ultimate mailing. Sound familiar? The perfect time to Test Before You Test!

So I designed a TBYT scenario using Google AdWords and facade testing. We built a one-page facade that talked about her product (vitamin supplements for building muscle and "bulking up"). The landing page included a web form to capture visitors' information (just in case anyone wanted to order, though that was not the goal).

Then we set up two pay-per-click ads using two different headlines that corresponded to the email subject lines she was planning to test later.

Audience: People who were interested in using vitamin supplements for building muscle.

Action: Clicking on a link to open a page with more information.

TBYT scenario: Both her email list and people searching for vitamin supplements would be similar, so we chose AdWords over Facebook.

Both clicking on an ad headline and clicking on an email subject line are similar behavior. So we had a valid behavioral context to test. We ran the headlines:

"Secrets to Building Body Mass"
"How to Build Your Body with Supplements"

All she had to do was test the two AdWords ads to see which one pulled the most number of clicks, then run with that headline as the subject line for her email campaign.

When we ran the ads, "Secrets..." had the better open rate even though it didn't even mention supplements. This was a surprise to our client, and made her glad she was testing before she tested. We were almost assured success if we sent the "Secrets..." subject line to more people on her email list.

She still wanted to test the second headline on her actual list, but she used it on a much smaller percentage of her list to maximize her success rates. 80% of the list received the "secrets" headline and 20% received the "how to" headline. If she had just guessed which headline was the best one, or split tested the campaign 50/50, she wouldn't have made nearly as much money as she did using our TBYT method.

With just $100 spent on AdWords, we had the results in 48 hours, and she could move forward with much more confidence about her success rates.

Pretty cool.

👍 GOOD TO KNOW

Maximizing Google AdWords

Google AdWords is a great tool to use for testing your audience. It's fast, and you can get vital data on actual consumer behavior in just a few hours. Unfortunately, it can be extremely expensive IF you try to figure it all out by yourself. Google assures its users that AdWords is simple and intuitive, and it is — if you want to pay Google full price.

There are so many ways to save a ton of money running an AdWords campaign. Basically, Google counts on most of its customers remaining ignorant of these techniques. Fortunately, you can get help from the world's foremost authority on AdWords, Perry Marshall.

Publisher's Description:
Double Your Web Traffic – Overnight!

Google gets searched more than 1 billion times every day — creating an unbelievable opportunity to get your business in front of thousands every minute…IF you know what you're doing.

Google AdWords experts, Perry Marshall and Bryan Todd, uncover the fundamentals, tech-

niques, tools, and tricks that Google should teach you, but doesn't.

Learn how to build an aggressive, streamlined campaign proven to increase your search engine visibility, consistently capture clicks and increase sales. No other guide is as comprehensive, or current in its coverage of today's fastest, most powerful advertising medium.

Invest $20 in his book, *The Ultimate Guide to Google AdWords*, and you'll be an expert user in no time. That tiny investment has saved me thousands of dollars in mistakes using AdWords.

For more information, check out
www.FailureisObsolete.com/adwords

What else can you use facade testing for?

How about testing book cover designs? Or even titles for your book? (I did this very test for the book you're reading right now.)

How about testing different prices for a certain product or service package?

You can test a design, business idea, new product, sales or marketing funnels — just about anything — using pay-per-click and Test Before You Test.

If you're concerned about damaging your company's reputation or promising things you can't deliver, remember you're only trying to test the concept or idea. You can build a facade for a brand you just made up out of the blue. Your test is to count the clicks, not to build the best website or have the actual products for sale.

As long as the landing page says "coming soon" or "request an invitation to join" or some other indication that the thing isn't ready yet, you're not doing any harm. You're just running an experiment on the ideal audience to see if your idea has any legs — is it worth the time, money, and energy that will need to go into building out the whole idea.

Remember, facade testing is not meant to be misleading. It's simply minimizing your risk. It keeps your budget low and your results quick. If you get a positive result on the facade, you can always go ahead and build out the entire website with your actual branding.

Conversion rate optimization is a whole science and art that is part analytics, part design, part creative think-

ing. It may take some time to get the hang of using split testing and Test Before You Test on your website or marketing funnel. But once you get used to it, you'll quickly become hooked on seeing better and better results show up with just small tweaks here and there (as long as they are the right tweaks).

If you run a business and have a website, you might want to read this chapter more than once.

THINGS TO REMEMBER

GOALS & ACTIONABLES

TBYT PRACTICE SHEET

Audience:

_____

_____

_____

Action:

_____

_____

_____

Test:

_____

_____

_____

_____

_____

_____

_____

5. LIFE

How to use the Test Before You Test strategy in your everyday decisions from dating to careers to retirement.

How to use the Test Before You Test strategy in your every day life to minimize risk, and prevent wasted time and energy.

It's probably easier to find ways to test ideas and decisions in business or on a website because it's not personal. It's not you. Surely human beings are above scientific testing and predicting successful outcomes, right?

Wrong.

Throughout this entire book we've been talking about creating experiments to predict human behavior. You've learned how to design low-risk tests to determine the likelihood of success on a higher-risk problem.

It works for your spouse, your kids, and your boss the same way it works for your business. (I know that may sound crazy, but stick with me here.)

In my opinion, life is all about maximizing happiness. If you agree, this chapter may be of great interest to you. To maximize happiness, you want to minimize the chances of making poor decisions that lead to less happy outcomes. You also want to minimize wasted energy, time, and money. Sound familiar? Perfect conditions for Test Before You Test.

Before we get too far, let me explain a little about historical data. Test Before You Test is all about running low-risk experiments to gather information (data) about something. When you use TBYT in your everyday life (as opposed to testing a new product or website idea) you already have access to all of recorded history to use as testing data.

History gives you free access to piles and piles of test data. Millions of experiments have already been proven in one way or another, you just have to access the results and apply them to your current situation. Sometimes accessing the data is instantaneous. Sometimes it takes a little research.

Should you say you're sorry when you hurt someone's feelings? Historical data says it could lead to a more successful outcome.

Should you head to a gas station when your car is running on fumes? Past experience (yours or someone else's) proves that's a good idea.

These are just silly, basic examples, but you get the point. There's an old saying, "Don't reinvent the wheel." It means "take the short cut" — learn from what others have already done and improve upon it.

Knowing the experiments that have come before you, and their outcomes, are as good or better than running your own experiments. Don't ignore the past. Study it and apply it to your own life. Using historical data and personal experience as the Test Before You Test lets you get on to the *real* test much faster.

For instance, you already know if you head out on a road trip with an empty gas tank, you're not going to get very far. So the decision to fill the tank first is fairly low-risk.

> But what about choosing your career?
> Asking the prom queen out on a date?
> Asking someone to marry you?
> Moving to another country?

All these higher-risk decisions require careful consideration. Unfortunately, you can spend way too much time deciding, and the opportunity passes you by. Remember what I said in the introduction about the future moving at the speed of thought? That means in your life as well.

The less time it takes you to make a committed decision, right or wrong, the faster you'll get to your destination. And if you know how to test high-risk propositions in a low-risk manner to predict recurring success — well, you'll be way ahead of everyone else.

Let's look at a few examples of how you can use the Test Before You Test strategy to make your life happier, healthier, and more meaningful overall. In other words, let's maximize happiness as fast as we can!

Example #1: Buying gifts for loved ones.
Let's start with an easy one. I'll bet you may have done some variation on this experiment in the past.

Imagine you want to buy your significant other something really, really special. Maybe you're even thinking she's "the one" and you don't want to mess this up. Your past experience tells you she would probably like a piece of jewelry. But what kind? What designer? Gold or silver (or leather)? Stones or no stones? You don't have a clue!

FIG 5.1: Creating maximum happiness - that's the goal. Even for something "normal" like choosing the perfect gift.

It's a perfect situation for Test Before You Test.

> **Same audience:** Your girlfriend
> **Same action:** Her face lights up at receiving jewelry as a gift

The high risk way to go about it (the way almost everyone does) is just get something you think is nice and hope for the best. That's trial and error, not a good predictor of success. You could also ask her friends what she likes.

But that's a survey, and we know how those tend to turn out.

Lower risk TBYT - Find excuses to show her several designers you think she'll like and note her reaction. (Casually, be smooth here, or you'll blow it.) That might be enough data to help you feel confident in your decision. But if you want more data, you could even purchase a small, inexpensive piece from that designer as a token gift for a smaller occasion (or for your mother or sister). If her reaction tests well, go ahead and purchase from that designer again for the more important occasion.

I've actually done this exact test on my wife, Jenna. (Don't worry, she knows I'm using this story.) When we were engaged to be married and I had already sweated bullets over choosing a ring for her, I was already planning ahead for our first anniversary. I knew I wanted to get her a really special piece of jewelry, but I didn't know what would make the "perfect" gift.

One day we were walking around downtown Washington D.C., and I pulled her into a fancy store (Michael Kors, if I recall correctly.) Jewelry was only one thing they had for sale at the store, so that was my way of being sneaky. We looked at bags and clothes and lots of different things. But then I gently guided her over to the jewelry counter and pointed out a certain piece I thought she'd like.

Her reaction: "Oh, no. I don't like that one. Ooh, but THAT one over there is beautiful!"

There was no occasion coming up, there was no reason for her to think I was fishing for gift ideas. One innocent little experiment and she told me everything about what she liked and didn't like without knowing I was keeping track.

This year, when our first anniversary came around, I used that test data to guide my choice for the perfect gift. I bought the piece she liked in the store all those months ago.

Her reaction was awesome! Her whole face lit up and she was so happy. Of course, I was thrilled that I had done so well picking out her gift. The TBYT experiment led to a successful outcome. Maximum happiness achieved!
Does it sound a little harsh to be testing gift purchases? Maybe. But you're seeking to create maximum happiness. The best chance of success. So why wouldn't you go about decisions in everyday life the same way you go about making business decisions?

I realize there are emotions at stake here, and you have to be more careful dealing with people's feelings. You might not want to actually tell your spouse or loved ones what you're doing. But the concept still remains. A little data gathering in the beginning goes a long way toward a happy ending. Let them wonder how you always manage to get the "perfect" gift.

Example #2: What day should you ask your boss for a raise?
I love this example because it happened to a friend of mine. He wanted to ask his boss for a raise, but wasn't sure when or how to do it. He wanted his boss to be in the best frame of mind to allow for the best possibility of getting a "yes." Really, what he wanted was to be able to predict a successful outcome. Time for a TBYT!

> **Audience:** The big boss.
> **Action:** Saying "yes" to a request.

The high-risk course of action would be to just ask for the extra money and hope for the best.

The lower-risk TBYT scenario was to ask for something smaller — like a day off, or some extra (non essential) supplies — on different days. Keep track of the response and notice the results.

Did he get a more favorable response on a Tuesday or a Friday?

Did he get a more favorable response by asking directly, or by buttering him up first?

Once you've gathered enough data to feel confident in your decision, you can predict the likelihood of a successful outcome. My friend did the TBYT and did wind up getting the raise. He totally deserved it, and he might have gotten it no matter what day he asked. But having a little behavioral context proof on his side made the decision easier.

FIG 5.2: Maximize your chances of getting that raise by making smaller requests first. How does the boss react? These are tests before you make the big test of asking for that raise.

Example #3: Choosing the right career.
Careers are tricky things. People choose their work in lots of different ways. They try to figure out what's going to make them the most money; give them the biggest adventure; have the most security; be the easiest interview; require the least amount of physical labor. Every person has his or her own ideas about their occupation.

But our culture rarely embraces the idea of choosing a career that will make us the most *happy*. Happiness might come into the equation at some point, but it's not usually the first consideration. (It turns out that could be a major mistake.)

Another consideration that can be overlooked is where you're most likely to be successful based on your natural strengths. I realize success means different things to different people. But no matter what your definition, success is something we can predict using the TBYT method.

These days people are pushed and prodded through high school and college before they really know what they are working towards. What's the goal, besides graduating and fulfilling some societal requirement?

Doesn't it make more sense to find out where you're likely to be successful and happy *before* you go spend $200,000 or more on a university degree that winds up having no value in your real life? More and more young people are figuring this out, and making smarter decisions about their lives early on.

I'm a huge believer in personality testing for finding out your own strengths and weaknesses. Will you be more successful in a management role or leadership?

FIG 5.3: For your best chance at success, test your career options *before* you spend four years and a boatload of money on a college degree.

Are you better at innovation and starting things quickly, or organizing and following things through to their conclusion? We all have different strengths and ways we deal with the world. And every industry needs people to fill lots of different types of roles.

You're going to be more successful, and ultimately happier, if you choose to do what you're naturally good at versus something you have to fight yourself to do.

If you're a natural leader who can come up with innovative ideas and ways to solve problems all day long, you're probably not going to be happy or successful stuck in middle management. If you love helping people finish projects or make their dreams become reality, you're going to be happier in an organizational or "follow-through" role. Helpers have a hard time being innovators.

👍 GOOD TO KNOW

Life, Liberty, and the Pursuit of Happiness

"We hold these truths to be self-evident, that all men are created equal, that they are endowed by their Creator with certain inalienable Rights, that among these are Life, Liberty and the pursuit of Happiness."
-Thomas Jefferson, The Declaration of Independence

Thomas Jefferson is something of a hero to me, more for his philosophy than his statesmanship. It's a hotly debated topic what Jefferson meant by "pursuit of Happiness." Was he talking about the rags to riches "American dream?" Or was he interested in a simpler kind of happiness — peace of mind and contentment? Personally, I think it was a little of both.

But what I truly admire about Jefferson's life is his love of efficiency and form. He was always looking for ways to improve upon known designs or invent new ways to accomplish necessary tasks. He was an experimenter, like me. His home at Monticello is jam-packed with inventions and uncommon items that improved efficiency, right down to the design of the building itself. Whenever I visit that famous house, I notice the most amazing things he invented or added to the house in the name of efficiency: revolving doors, the carefully planned gardens, and a small dumbwaiter on the sides of his fireplace specifically for transporting wine from the cellar below without making the trip (see picture below).

I like to think we would get along well, and that Jefferson would be great at conversion rate optimization.

 For more information, check out
www.FailureisObsolete.com/jefferson

No personality type is better or worse than any other. It's just the way you do things. And when you know this in advance (through testing) you can choose occupations and careers that make you happy and successful.

> **Audience:** You.
> **Action:** Experiencing success doing certain types of tasks (innovation/follow-through, outdoor/indoor, manual labor/desk job, etc).

High-risk scenario — get a college degree in something your parents told you would be a good choice, then get a job (if you can) and hope for the best.

The lower-risk TBYT scenario — Before you go out looking for a certain job or getting a college degree, gather some data. Do some tests on your own behavior. Find out what types of activities you naturally excel in. (I highly recommend taking the KOLBE A test online as a starting point.) Then look for some lower-risk short term activities that simulate the activities you think will suit you.

I did just that the summer I turned 18, before I went off to college. I already had a small computer business where I helped people set up networks in their homes, ran wires for them, did tech support, etc. It was kind of like the "Geek Squad" at those big box computer stores, but it was just a few employees and me.

I really enjoyed what I was doing, and thought I would go into computer science in college. But just to make sure I was taking the right path, I also took on a low-paying tech support job at a local Fortune 500 company. The idea was to see how I would like working in a big corporation doing the same kinds of things I was doing on my own.

It was miserable! No one there was happy, not even my superiors. I didn't enjoy my work, and I really couldn't see myself working this type of job for the rest of my life. What I learned was that IT people are basically fixing things, not creating things. I was a creator, which is why I enjoyed running my own business.

Thank goodness I ran that experiment! There's no telling how much time, energy, and money it saved me. I went to school, immediately changed my major from computer science to business, and I've been happy with that choice ever since. Computers are still at the core of my work, but I am creating things, and I am in charge of my own destiny. Maximum happiness achieved.

👍 GOOD TO KNOW

Personality Testing as a Form of TBYT

Most people go through life just fine without ever thinking about their personality traits. But if you take the time to test where your natural strengths and weaknesses lie, you can use that data to create more success in your career and your personal life.

It's a form of testing before you test. You are testing for natural inclinations in a low-risk environment, so you can set yourself up for success when the real high-risk tests come (like marriage, children, starting a business, etc.).

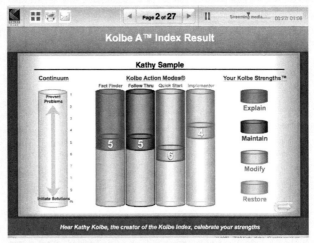

Fig 5.4: The Kolbe A Index identifies and measures your natural talents. Working with your strengths sets you up for success in life.

One of my favorite tools for this kind of testing is called the Kolbe test. I've taken it many times, and I have all my employees take it, too. As a business owner, it helps me work within my strengths. It also helps me understand how my employees work best, so I can set them up for a successful, happy working relationship. You can learn more about the Kolbe test at the web page listed below.

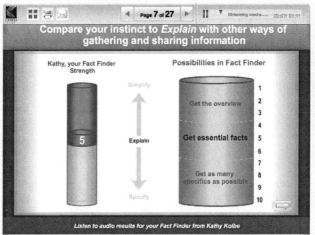

Fig 5.5: Running your employees (or even your kids) through the Kolbe test helps you give them assignments and tasks they will naturally excel in. Success keeps everybody happy!

For more information, check out
www.FailureisObsolete.com/kolbe

Example #4: Dating and Marriage.

How do you find that special someone you might be interested in spending your life with?

In the old days, your parents decided for you. Or you simply married the first person who asked and hoped for the best. Those methods obviously present a high risk of failure. (Of course, even if there is no option for failure - no divorce allowed by law - then there is at least a high risk for a miserable life.)

These days you date people before entering into a high-risk marriage proposition. Dating is the test. But dating takes lots of time, energy, money, and emotional investment. It can also be a high-risk proposition. So high risk, in fact, that one bad experience can make people afraid to try again, or make them guard their emotions carefully so they are never hurt like that again. But very few people get it right the first time, so they have to risk that hurt over and over until they eventually get it right.

Maybe.

If they're lucky.

In theory, we should all learn from the mistakes made in our bad relationships and continually improve in future efforts. Unfortunately, the real world doesn't seem to work that way. We blunder around, making the same mistakes over and over and consider ourselves "lucky" if we do manage to find and stay with the right person.

But could we somehow lessen the risk of wasted energy and emotional pain *before* we get involved in a messy relationship? Is there some way to learn about a person's *true behaviors* before we waste too much time? (Sounds like a perfect chance for a TBYT, don't you think?)

Data gathering, or testing before you test, before you even start dating someone is a great way to learn about them in a low-risk setting. One way to do that is to become friends with the person first. Taking a long-term friendship into an even longer-term love affair is the stuff of legend and fairy tales. It does happen, but it takes a long time and a fair amount of luck. And many of us are stuck in relatively small social circles, so it can be difficult to strike up friendships with compatible people.

Enter online dating.
The dating world has changed dramatically with the advent of online and speed dating. When you join a group like eHarmony, you are radically enlarging your circle of available people to strike up conversations and friendships with. Through an honest use of your profile, you can weed out unsuitable candidates quickly and only connect with people who meet your criteria.

eHarmony figured out that if people could use technology to do research and start interacting with others before even starting the dating process. People were more likely to have successful relationships with this "pre-dating" model. It's a Test Before You Test model — simulating behavior in a high-risk situation using less personal interfaces. It's difficult to go on a date and then disentangle yourself from someone easily if they live in your neighborhood, work at your office, hang out with your close friends, etc. You're almost obligated to "give it a try" longer than you may want to. But in a simple online chat scenario, you can continue the conversation as long as you want to. And if you decide it's not going anywhere, you can end it with the click of a button. No mess.

So how can you use TBYT to get the most accurate results when you're chatting with a potential date?

What you don't want to do is turn your chat time into a survey. Yes/No questions don't provide much data, and people can easily say what they think you want to hear. This is why classified ads don't work well. They are basically surveys in disguise. (Do you like Pina Coladas? Check. How about getting caught in the rain?)

Instead, you want to ask open-ended interrogative questions. An interrogative sentence is one that starts with words like who, what, when, where, why, and how. Let's say you're looking for a fellow tennis fanatic. (It's a tough game to play alone.) What are some good ways to gather data?

Instead of asking, "Do you like tennis?"
Ask, "What's your favorite pastime?" or "What's your favorite sport?" or "When you have a weekend free, what do you like to do?"

Can you see how interrogatives lead to more discovery? They leave room for almost any answer at all. If the person responds "I love a competitive game of tennis on a Saturday morning," you might have a good match. If they say, "Reading is all I do on the weekends", you might not have a good match. But then again, you might… you have to get more information.

You're data gathering.

FIG 5.6: Asking the right questions can give you better data. Instead of asking , "Do you like tennis?" (survey) Try asking, "What do you like to do on the weekends?" If the answer is, "I love a good game of tennis on the weekends" then you've got more reliable data and can move forward with confidence.

The questions you ask and how they answer gives you the data to help you predict a successful outcome. They help you decide if you want to take the next step of going on an actual date.

If the desired behavior you're looking for on a date is someone who is easy to talk to, and with whom you have common interests, then simply use your TBYT chat time to find out if that's how they behave when you're chatting. Online chat is the low-risk TBYT for the higher-risk date. And the dating time is ultimately a TBYT for marriage or a long-term commitment.

Of course, there are no guarantees. People change. Sometimes they behave differently according to what's going on in their lives. It's not foolproof.

I'm not suggesting you think about people's emotions as mere data points on a graph. I am suggesting it's better than going in blind, or setting yourself up for repeated disappointments. And it's a great way to learn something about yourself in the process, and keep from repeating the same mistakes over and over again. It's maximizing happiness.

Example #5: Buying a house.
A house is a huge investment, financially and emotionally. Yet many people just look around at houses in their price range, pick one, and hope for the best. Other people put so much effort into finding the "perfect" house, in the "perfect" neighborhood, near the "best" schools, only to discover what they thought they wanted most turns out to be wrong.

For example, I used to think I wanted a big green lawn in front of my house, and a huge back yard. That is, until I had to spend a significant portion of my Saturdays mowing grass. Now, I'm content with a smaller green space that someone else gets to trim.

It's fairly simple to design a TBYT scenario for new home buyers, but you have to spend a little time thinking about it ahead of time. And you have to be willing to put off the actual purchase for a while.

> **Audience:** You.
> **Action:** Being blissfully happy in your dream home with the XYZ.

The XYZ is what you have to define. What is most important to you? Do you want a large yard with a backyard swimming pool? Do you want a gourmet kitchen and room for entertaining? Is it important that you not be too near your neighbors? Or would you prefer a nice small bungalow that's private and easy to clean? How far do you have to commute to work? Can you walk to the grocery store?

Figure out the most important features for you and then rent at least two houses before you buy. The first rental is the TBYT. You're data gathering. Did you *actually* want what you thought you wanted? How happy are you in that small, easy-to-clean space? Do you love that swimming pool, or do you find you never really use it?

Next, you'll want to rent a second house with your revised vision. This is the actual test. Are you happy here, with these features?

Of course, it may not be feasible to spend two or more years trying to figure out the best house for you. But the idea is still sound. Could you housesit for someone with a home similar to the kind you're thinking of? Or maybe spend a few weeks in a vacation rental that matches your desired features?

The length of time you spend gathering data isn't as important as monitoring your "happy levels" while you're there. Take the data gathering seriously. If you think you want to live on a farm, but you've only ever seen them in the movies, you might want to think seriously about a test. Stay on a working farm before you invest a lot of time, energy, and money into a venture you wind up hating. The same goes for living in the noisy city when all you've ever known is the peace and quiet of the countryside.

You can also shortcut the TBYT phase by keeping track of

all the things you truly like or dislike about all the temporary living situations you find yourself in before you buy a house. This is data gathering on the fly. But you have to be honest with yourself, and it's wise to test living the opposite way to be sure you're getting accurate data.

It's really easy to fool yourself — like wanting to live alone when you're used to having roommates. This one is very common. All you think about when you have roommates is how great it will be having a place all to yourself. Then when you finally get your own place, you find out how lonely it can be.

Example #6: Retirement.

Everyone looks forward to retirement, right? Those golden years of relaxing on the front porch, playing golf whenever

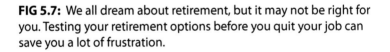

FIG 5.7: We all dream about retirement, but it may not be right for you. Testing your retirement options before you quit your job can save you a lot of frustration.

we want to, taking cruises, or gardening the day away…

I'm a young guy, so it may seem odd that I'm talking about retirement, but stick with me. See, I always thought I would retire early and live the "easy life." But now after running experiments like the ones below, I know that the reality is I'll probably never retire. I'm too happy being busy, and I can't stand having nothing to do. It makes me crazy!

These days, people are finding that the old-fashioned notion of retirement isn't all it's cracked up to be. People need to feel useful, to feel like they have a reason to get up in the morning. And without a regular job to go to, they can feel lost and depression can set in.

So, how can you tell if you'll enjoy an active, vital retirement, or whether you might be better off just finding a different job? Quitting and hoping for the best is one way. But not the way I would recommend. It's just another high-risk situation that calls for a lower-risk test scenario.

> **Audience:** You.
> **Action:** Enjoying unscheduled days for long periods of time.

How could you simulate retirement without actually quitting your job? An extended vacation or leave-of-absence would do nicely. I'm not suggesting a vacation where you have travel plans or family visiting or a big fancy holiday to distract you, but rather a vacation where you stay home and simulate what retirement would actually be like.

Then start gathering data:

> — How would you fill your days?
> — Do you get bored within the first few hours of rising?
> — Are you eager to get up and start your day? Or do you find yourself sleeping more, just to pass the time?
> — Do you continue learning new things? Do you start up a new hobby?

— Do you surround yourself with friends, or do you isolate yourself?

— Are you comfortable with the amount of money you have available to live on?

A second valid data-gathering activity would be to try out a different occupation during your extended vacation to simulate changing jobs rather than retiring. Maybe volunteer your time at an organization that does work in a field you're interested in. Not only will you be able to test out the new field in a low-risk way, you'll also be making friends who could open doors for you if you did decide to make the change permanent.

Testing before you test in your own life is all about being honest with yourself and becoming a good objective observer of situations and how they make you feel.

It's not easy, that's for sure. Your mind can play tricks on you. Friends and family can persuade you along different paths. Your past experiences can make you reluctant to try new or different experiences. And your emotions are a huge component that are hard to predict.

Some of this may seem so obvious it's painful, and not every situation is going to need a TBYT scenario. The big idea is to think "test before you act" whenever you can — even if it's just a single test. Testing helps you make more successful decisions, more often.

Take it one step at a time, seek to exchange high-risk propositions for lower-risk tests and record the results. You'll be able to predict successful outcomes more and more often.

THINGS TO REMEMBER

GOALS & ACTIONABLES

TBYT PRACTICE SHEET

Audience:

_____
_____
_____
_____

Action:

_____
_____
_____
_____

Test:

_____
_____
_____
_____
_____
_____
_____

6. CONCLUSION

If there's only one thing you take away from this book, this is it.

At the end of all my consulting sessions, I like to leave my clients with something important and actionable, in case the session was overwhelming. I always wrap up by saying, "If there's only one thing you take away from all this, here it is..."

So, if there's one thing you take away from this book, it's this: Don't get wound up in the details and the unfamiliar words. The whole idea behind the last 160 pages or so is to minimize risk and maximize happiness in all areas of your life and business.

If the Test Before You Test strategy seems overwhelming, remember you don't have to do it all. You don't have to do it perfectly either. But it's healthy and smart to think about your behavior. What are the options you have when making decisions? Are you taking an unnecessarily high risk? Or could you run a cheap test quickly to see if your idea is likely to succeed (to see if you're making the best decision before you even make it)?

People who aren't close friends with me might think I'm a big risk-taker because of the companies I start from nothing and how I invest my money. But the truth is, I am relatively risk averse. The trick is I rarely need to take big risks because I almost always have direct evidence of the pending outcome. So my choices may seem risky, but because of TBYT and the way I look at the world, they almost never are.

If you integrate this thought process into your life, don't be surprised if you soon find yourself clocking more successes and bigger wins than ever.

Remember, all you have to do to run a TBYT experiment is to have the same audience and the same action for both the low and high-risk situations. Even if the test isn't perfect, it's better than going out there blind and hoping for the best.

I wish you all the best of success and happiness in your life and business!

REFERENCE LIST

Here's a quick list of all the website links found in this book.

www.FailureisObsolete.com/Infusionsoft — For more information on Infusionsoft, my favorite all-in-one CRM/Email marketing/eCommerce software.

www.FailureisObsolete.com/email-equation — For more information about my equation for successful email marketing.

www.FailureisObsolete.com/teen-entrepreneurs — For more information about the trend toward teen entrepreneurs.

www.FailureisObsolete.com/self-perception — For more information about the psychological theory of self-perception.

www.FailureisObsolete.com/virtual-company — For a list of tools and tips for running a virtual company.

www.FailureisObsolete.com/unbounce — For an easy to use web-building platform.

www.FailureisObsolete.com/meetup — For more details about using Meetup.com for testing and hosting live events.

www.FailureisObsolete.com/non-profit — For more information on how non-profits can use Test Before You Test.

www.FailureisObsolete.com/click-through-rate — For more information on what a click-through-rate is and why it's an important piece of data for any business or organizational website.

www.FailureisObsolete.com/adwords — For more information on Perry Marshall's *The Ultimate Guide to Google AdWords*.

www.FailureisObsolete.com/Facebook — For more information on the book *The Ultimate Guide to Facebook Advertising*.

www.FailureisObsolete.com/split-testing — For more information on how to use split-testing on your website.

www.FailureisObsolete.com/conversion-tools — For more information on tools you can use for conversion rate optimization.

www.FailureisObsolete.com/kolbe — For more information on the Kolbe personality testing I use for my employees and myself.

www.FailureisObsolete.com/jefferson — For more information on Thomas Jefferson's home, Monticello, and how he implemented efficiency into the design of the house.

www.AvenueInnBB.com — For more information about an awesome bed and breakfast in the heart of New Orleans (my parents' inn).

www.FailureisObsolete.com/reference-list — For a complete list of the links mentioned on the Failure is Obsolete member website.

YOU'RE INVITED!

Come join our community of reverse engineers and experimenters.

As a reader, you're entitled to a free membership on our website —

www.FailureisObsolete.com/member

When you sign up, you'll get bonus tips, added resources, practice pages, and more.

It takes seconds to sign up.

Just go to www.FailureisObsolete.com/member and fill out the short free membership form.

NOTES

NOTES

NOTES

NOTES